Library of
Davidson College

THE NEUTRAL GROUND

Engraving of Major André by W. Jackman. Reproduced from the original in the Henry E. Huntington Library and Art Gallery, San Marino, California. Reprinted by permission.

THE NEUTRAL GROUND

The André Affair and the Background of Cooper's *The Spy*

BRUCE A. ROSENBERG

Contributions to the Study of Popular Culture, Number 42

GREENWOOD PRESS
Westport, Connecticut • London

Library of Congress Cataloging-in-Publication Data

Rosenberg, Bruce A.
    The neutral ground : the André affair and the background of Cooper's The spy / Bruce A. Rosenberg.
      p. cm.—(Contributions to the study of popular culture, ISSN 0198–9871 ; no. 42)
    Includes bibliographical references and index.
    ISBN 0–313–29319–8 (alk. paper)
    1. Cooper, James Fenimore, 1789–1851. Spy. 2. United States—History—Revolution, 1775–1783—Literature and the revolution. 3. Historical fiction, American—History and criticism. 4. Spy stories, American—History and criticism. 5. André, John, 1751–1780—In literature. 6. Espionage in literature. 7. Spies in literature. I. Title. II. Series.
PS1417.S72R67 1994
813'.2—dc20   94–16127

British Library Cataloguing in Publication Data is available.

Copyright © 1994 by Bruce A. Rosenberg

All rights reserved. No portion of this book may be reproduced, by any process or technique, without the express written consent of the publisher.

Library of Congress Catalog Card Number: 94–16127
ISBN: 0–313–29319–8
ISSN: 0198–9871

First published in 1994

Greenwood Press, 88 Post Road West, Westport, CT 06881
An imprint of Greenwood Publishing Group, Inc.

Printed in the United States of America

The paper used in this book complies with the Permanent Paper Standard issued by the National Information Standards Organization (Z39.48–1984).

10 9 8 7 6 5 4 3 2 1

For Ann

Contents

Acknowledgments ix

PART I. MAJOR ANDRÉ

1. Hanging Is for Spies 3
2. The Gentleman's Code 9
3. The Blackest Treason 15
4. A Gentleman's Education 19
5. The Arnold Enlistment 27
6. This Is a Spy! 41
7. Posthumous Encomia 51

PART II. JAMES FENIMORE COOPER

8. The André Affair and *The Spy* 63
9. André and Cooper 73
10. Cooper and the Spy Novel 83
11. The McDonald Papers 87
12. The Neutral Ground 95

PART III. *THE SPY*

    13. An American Novel 105

    14. Dramatis Personae 113

    15. The Neutral Ground 135

References 147

Index 153

Acknowledgments

I wish to thank the following individuals and institutions for their support of this project. Dr. & Mrs. (Steven and Carol) Wallach. Stacy Wallach. Prof. John Cawelti. Prof. Barton Levi St. Armand. Prof. Ann Harleman. Gordon Bakken. Ms. Barbara Donagan. Prof. Joyce Malcolm. The Huntington Library; the Committee on Research, Prof. Martin Ridge, Chairman. Virginia Renner. Susan Naulte (Assistant Curator, Rare Book Department). Tom Lange. Mary Wright. Prof. Jas. Thorpe. Brown University Office of Grants and Research (for a seed grant). The Huguenot Historical Society.

Part One

MAJOR ANDRÉ

1

Hanging Is for Spies

Mabie Tavern, Tappan, New York. This public house was one of the few secure buildings in this small village, the site of Major André's incarceration and trial; nearby, General Washington had established his headquarters, and a sizable force of the Continental Army was encamped there. On the morning of 2 October 1780, Major John André breakfasted at eight on food sent from Washington's mess. After he had finished he was told the hour, but not the mode, of his execution. He is said—by Dr. James Thatcher, Continental Army surgeon, who was there—to have received the news "without emotion" (*Andreana* 1865, pp. 58ff.). Then he carefully, creaselessly, dressed himself in his fresh regimentals, "with as much composure as though he were going to a ball" (Hatch 1986, p. 272). All the others present were "affected with silent gloom" (*Andreana* 1865, pp 58ff.). Earlier, his tunic had been brought from New York City along with fresh linens, by Peter Laune, his batman. He was an officer of the Fifty-Fourth, and would proudly proclaim it on that day to all of his surrounding enemies. If he was nervous or fearful there is no record of it. A moment of dramatic and didactic contrast followed: Laune could not remain composed throughout this preliminary drama, and was brusquely rebuked by his superior: "Leave me till you can show yourself more manly" (from Dr. Thatcher's journal in *Andreana 1865*, pp. 58ff.).

Yet if this is high tragedy, these nearly last words do not ring quite true; perhaps tragedy is the wrong genre. For, as

Hatch has it (1986, pp. 271ff.), André slept little on his last night. When Laune brought him his tunic and asked if he could do anything else, the Major, who seemed on the verge of tears, is said to have answered, "You have done well. You have done well." By dawn he had pulled himself together, and so that earlier episode has to be seen as a grimly ironic anticipation of his final demonstration of strength. When those around him were moved to pity for his sake, he would gather his courage and show himself a model of self-possessed bravery.

Even at this late moment, when Colonel Alexander Scammel entered his chamber to inform him that he was to be executed at noon, André was not certain how he would die, by noose or musket ball, but he did have the confidence that his recent letter to General Washington would be effective. The mode was important to him. Why would His Excellency, himself a man of honor, refuse this request of a doomed man? Major André had made the reasonable request of one gentleman, one soldier, to another: "sympathy towards a soldier will surely induce your Excellency and a military tribunal to adopt the mode of my death to the feeling of a man of honor ... by being informed that I am not to die on a gibbet" (letter of John André to George Washington, 1 Oct. 1780).

Washington's aide, Alexander Hamilton, was surprised at his commander's failure to respond to what seemed to him a gentlemanly request. He is said to have remarked to his fiancée, Elizabeth Schuyler, that since André was doomed, he should at least be allowed to choose the method of his destruction. Hope for an execution appropriate for a gentleman fluttered momentarily when the sentence was delayed a day. The adjutant general of the British army spent these last few hours sketching with pen and ink; one of his drawings was of himself being rowed ashore from HMS *Vulture*—the operational beginning of this disastrous mission. Laune took it back to headquarters in New York for him. A self-portrait was given to one of his guards. But what could have been in his mind with such a gesture? The desire of a gentleman who wanted one of his socially inferior captors to remember him, and to remember admiringly a very brave and composed officer and gentleman who spent his last hours in such casual pursuits? How better to manifest his acceptance of his fate on the verge of his death? He became the martyr who wanted to immortalize himself by the skills of his own hand.

On the morning of 2 October 1780, carpenters began to dress and assemble a gallows, while the curious gathered from around the countryside, not only from New Jersey and New York, but from as far away as Pennsylvania. Dr. Thatcher observed that "an immense concourse of people assembled." They had invited themselves to a hanging. "Melancholy and gloom pervaded all ranks, and the scene was affectingly awful" (*Andreana* 1865, p. 59). An armed detachment assembled outside the tavern, and the music of an accompanying fife-and-drum unit signaled that the moment had come. André is said to have remarked calmly to his (officer) guards that he was "ready at any moment, gentlemen, to wait on you" (Decker 1959, p. 116).

As he stepped out of his prison door, all eyes were fixed upon him; Dr. Thatcher remarks (*Andreana* 1865, p. 59) that he rose "superior to the fears of death [and] appeared as if conscious of the dignified deportment which he displayed."

One member of the crowd, an artificer in Colonel Jeduthun Baldwin's regiment, later recalled details that others had not noticed or did not bother recording; André "had a long and beautiful head of hair"; and it was generally believed of his bearing at the time that no officer in the British army, similarly circumstanced, "would have appeared better than this unfortunate man" (William Keeney Bixby Collection in the Huntington Library, #X 68034).

Once within the parade to the (still unknown to him) gallows, André further remarked on matters nearly extraneous: "I am very much surprised to find your troops under such good discipline, and your music is excellent." André marched with his guards as though to a wedding, nodding and smiling in recognition of certain known Continental officers. "He betrayed no want of fortitude, but retained a complacent smile on his countenance" (*Andreana* 1865, p. 59).

The killing field was more than a mile from Mabie Tavern. André marched the distance cheerfully, his escort more somberly. But when the road topped a hill and veered to the left, André saw for the first time the gallows in the middle of a field choked with the curious. He is said to have been taken aback: "Gentlemen, I am disappointed" (Hatch 1986, p. 273). An officer near him asked this curious question under the circumstances: "Why the emotion, Sir?" Whether it happened this way or not, the question did give André the opportunity to reply with one of the important lines of the moment: "I am reconciled to my death, but detest the mode" (Decker 1959, p. 117). Major Benjamin Russell recalled that the captain commanding the inner guard responded, "It is unavoidable, Sir" (*Andreana* 1865, pp. 62-64).

André marched passed the Board of General Officers as they stood near the gallows. And, in what was a very great display of forgiving courage, bowed respectfully to each in turn. General Washington and his staff were not present—a mark of decorum, thought Major Russell (*Andreana* 1865, pp. 62-64), that was "feelingly appreciated by the sufferer." One of the audience, medical inspector Dr. John Hart, was overwhelmed by the gesture: "such fortitude I never was witness of" (Hatch 1986, p. 273). The officer of the day, Colonel Scammel, and Peter Laune stood by the scaffold, Laune now once again weeping. André asked to meet with Benjamin Tallmadge—the officer who had the most to do with his incarceration, after all—and when the American stepped forward André grasped his hand and shook it firmly.

Dr. Thatcher recorded in his journal that while standing close to the gibbet, he noticed that the major seemed to have difficulty swallowing; there was a "choking in his throat." His foot nervously fondled a stone (Flexner 1953, p. 392; *Andreana* 1865, pp. 58-61). Thatcher observed "some degree of trepidation." Then the condemned man stepped to the victim's wagon, elevated his head, and murmured, "It will be but a momentary pang" (Decker 1959, p. 117). He took off his handkerchief and gave it to Laune, who had again lost emotional control. With a handkerchief from his own pocket he blindfolded himself, heard the death sentence read by Colonel Scammel, who asked if he had anything to say, then called to those near: "I have nothing more than this, that I would have you gentlemen bear me witness that I die like a brave man" (Hatch 1986, p. 274). Dr. Thatcher commented in his journal that "it was a tragical scene of the deepest interest" (*Andreana* 1865, pp. 58 ff.)

One more gesture of sublime poise remained; when the hangman stepped forward and tried to place the noose over the major's head and around his neck, André took the rope from him and placed it over his neck himself, drawing the knot firmly. Some low comedy intervened when the major, who had removed the handkerchief when placing the rope, now blindfolded himself again, only to have the presiding officer blurt out that his hands had to be tied. André removed another handkerchief from his pocket and handed it to his executioner, who secured his arms behind him.

All the details now accounted for, the hangman, who had blackened his face to avoid being identified, jumped down from the cart; at the crack of a whip the horses snapped forward, the wagon lurched from under the prisoner, and the major was left hanging. Minutes later, amidst a mainly sorrowful crowd, Dr. Timothy Hull pronounced him dead (Decker 1959, p. 118). Again, Colonel Baldwin's artificer remembers details that others neglected, in this case morbid ones. After André's body was placed in its coffin, an (anonymous) soldier moved forward through the crowd to examine it. André had been left hanging for twenty to thirty minutes. In the coffin, André's head "was very much on one side . . . . His face appeared to be greatly swollen and very black" (Bixby Collection, Huntington Library #X 68034).

2

The Gentleman's Code

Consistent with the gentleman's code of the day, prisoner André had been in direct touch with his jailer, General Washington. On 24 September he wrote to the general, arguing his case:

> I am too little accustomed to duplicity to have succeeded .... The person in your possession *is* Major John André, Adjutant-General to the British army .... I agreed to meet upon ground not within posts of either army, a person who was to give me intelligence. (*Andreana* 1865, pp. 9-13)

Shrewdly, he avoided any inflammatory mention of Arnold's name, thus protecting his collaborator in case the treasonous general had not made an escape, and avoiding the retributive wrath of the colonials if he had; André recognized that they were likely to be enraged by Arnold's treason:

> I came up in the Vulture man of war for this effect, and was fetched by a boat from the shore to the beach. Being there I was told that the approach of day would prevent my return, and that I must be concealed until the next night. I was in my regimentals and had fairly risked my person. Against my stipulation, my intention and without my knowledge before hand, I was conducted within one of your posts. Your Excellency [referred to as "Mr." Washington in private correspondence and conversations] may conceive my sensation on this occasion and will imagine how much more I must have been affected, by a refusal to reconduct me back the next night as I had been brought. Thus become a prisoner I had to concert my escape. I quitted my uniform and was passed another way in the night without the American posts to neutral ground, and informed I was beyond all armed parties and left to press for New York. I was taken at Tarry Town by some volunteers. Thus as I have had the honor to relate was I

> betrayed (being Adjutant General of the British army) into the vile condition of an enemy in disguise within your posts. Having avowed myself a British officer I have nothing to reveal but what relates to myself, which is true on the honor of an officer and a gentleman ... the request I have to make ... [is] that though unfortunate I am branded with nothing dishonorabler, as no motive could be mine but the service of my king and as I was involuntarily an impostor. (*Andreana* 1865, pp. 9-13)

André's defense is essentially "no contest"; he admits to the actions which are the bases of the charges being brought against him. But he feels that he has been involuntarily placed in a compromising position by circumstances and personnel outside of his control and authority. He had been caught out of uniform against his will and inclination. As a gentleman of honor he appeals to Washington, another officer and gentleman, to pardon him this embarrassing misdemeanor, this awkward circumstance he is now in. The commander of the colonial armies, however, was not persuaded.

From Robinson's house ("in the highlands") Washington reported on 26 September to the "President of the Congress":

> Sir,
>
> > I have the honor to inform Congress that I arrived here yesterday about twelve o'clock, on my return from Hartford. Some hours previous to my arrival, Major-General Arnold went from his quarters, which were this place, and, as it was supposed, over the river to the garrison at West Point, whither I proceeded myself, in order to visit the post. I found General Arnold had not been there during the day; and, on my return to his quarters, he was still absent. In the meantime, a packet had arrived from Lieut. Colonel Jameson, announcing the capture of a John Anderson, who was endeavoring to go to New York, with several interesting and important papers, all in the hand-writing of General Arnold. This was accompanied with a letter from the prisoner, avowing himself to be Major John André, Adjutant-General to the British army, relating the manner of his capture, and endeavoring to show that he did not come under the description of a spy. From these several circumstances, and information that the general seemed to be thrown into some degree of agitation, on receiving a letter a little time before he went from his quarters, I was led to conclude

immediately that he had heard of Major André's captivity, and that he would, if possible, escape to the enemy; and accordingly took such measures as appeared the most probable to apprehend him. But he had embarked in a barge, and proceeded down the river, under a flag, to the Vulture ship of war. (*Andreana* 1865, pp. 3-4)

Washington almost immediately convened a Board of General Officers: a high-powered board, it consisted of all of the general officers at Headquarters, including among its fourteen generals Lafayette, von Steuben, and Nathaniel Greene, and so charged them:

Gentlemen,

Major André, Adjutant General to the British Army, will be brought before you for your examination. He came within our lines in the night, on an interview with Major General Arnold, and in an assumed character; and was taken within our lines, in a disguised habit, with a pass under a feigned name, and with the enclosed papers concealed upon him. After a careful examination you will be pleased as speedily as possible, to report a precise state of his case, together with your opinion of the light in which he ought to be considered, and the punishment that ought to be inflicted. The Judge-Advocate will attend to attest in the examination, who has sundry other papers, relative to this matter, which he will lay before the Board. (*Andreana* 1865, pp. 8-9)

Washington's charge was, naturally enough, as prejudicial to André's case as was his own admission. The false pass under a "feigned name" and "the disguised habit" are given prominence, as is—quite properly—the "enclosed papers," which are the elements of the specific and concrete evidence against André and Arnold. The tone of Washington's charge to the board implies the desired decision. During its examination, board members asked him if he had in fact crossed American lines at night and under a false name. Did he have in his possession a pass made out to a "John Anderson"? Was he dressed in civilian attire during his attempt to return to British lines? And did he have, concealed on his person, papers and maps in Benedict Arnold's handwriting bespeaking espionage? One highlight was André's refusal to claim that he had begun his mission "under the protection of a flag." If he had, André readily pointed out, he most certainly would have returned to his own lines under the same sanction. The General Board presumably did not accept André's contention that he had been made a prisoner of war; subsequent apologists have argued that André entered American lines under the sanction of a flag, a defense that he himself seems to have disdained. He did act under the orders of a superior officer, but that officer was contemplating treason, and André was under no legal obligation to obey him (Flexner 1953, p. 384). A few days later, the board reported back to Washington, echoing the language of several of his most damning charges:

> that he changed his dress within our lines, and under a feigned name, and in a disguised habit, passed our works at Stoney and Verplank's Points, ... and when taken, he had in his possession several papers, which contained intelligence for the enemy .... The Board having maturely considered these facts, do also report ... that Major André ... ought to be considered as a spy from the enemy and ... it is their opinion, he ought to suffer death.

In a less emotional time the board and its decision (and Washington's) could certainly be challenged. The British and the Continental Armies did not operate under any codified rules of war; the Hague and, later, Geneva Conventions, were more than a century away.

The British army, at least, had some written moral guidelines, though, not quite relevant to André's situation—*Laws and Ordinances of Warre, Established for the better Conduct of the ARMY,* compiled by the Earl of Essex in 1643: whosoever shall come from the enemy without a trumpet or drum, after the custom of war, within the quarters of the army or a garrison town, shall be hanged as a spy (1643, n.p.). But this document says nothing about defining the status of a spy, or whether the accepted and usual punishment for captured spies was hanging. Though spies were used throughout the English Civil War, they were not a common enough occurrence to merit legal (or moral) commentary. Nations, and armies, behaved according to what they, and that great jurist, Hugo Grotius, termed the Law of Nations and the Law of Arms:

> Everything is lawful that is done against an Enemy; and all Conquerours are more or less severe, according as it shall

conduce to their future advantage, for thus are spies dealt withal; yet not withstanding, it is held lawful by the general consent of Nations, to send out such, as *Moses* did *Joshua* into the land of *Caanan*. It is the custom of all nations to kill spies ... and that justly sometimes by such as have apparently a just Cause to make War. (III, p. 463)

Grotius' expert legal predecessor, Robert Ward (1639), had nothing to say about spies or espionage in his *Animadversions of Warre*. This silence is significant, but what does it mean? That spies were not consequential enough to mention in a volume of the conduct of warfare? That espionage was a distasteful subject never mentioned in print? That spying was too clandestine a matter to discuss openly? In any event, after Grotius' legal treatise of 1682, the unwritten agreements of nations had been made more specific, and more precisely covered situations such as André's. Yet they were still unwritten. According to the prevailing customs of the conduct of warfare in the late eighteenth century, a spy is someone who clandestinely seeks information within an area controlled by the enemy, with the intent of transmitting such information to the "other side." True, André was out of uniform, but that in itself is not criminal. He was not captured within the enemy's territory, but was, as I have stressed, on neutral ground. And it is questionable whether he dissimulated or acted in bad faith.

Nevertheless, such fine points were skimmed over by the board (if, in fact, they were ever aware of such distinctions) because if André had not himself acted in bad faith, he had certainly communicated with and abetted one who had. As Colonel C. Dewitt Willcox, professor of military law at West Point, has concluded (Sargent, *Journal* 1904, p. 125), André's mission was lawful (according to the contemporary understanding of the rules of warfare); he got caught, however, and his co-conspirator was instantly so deeply hated that he, André, guilty by association, paid the price.

Curiously, André never pressed the detail of his having been captured outside of the American lines (neither did General Clinton in his communications with Washington), or of the lawfulness of his mission—though he did hint at the latter. But then, André was not a lawyer, and had not been trained in the law. Even if he had, it might not have made much difference, determined as the Americans were to avenge themselves for Arnold's defection and to ensure that no American would ever be tempted to emulate the traitor. As Alexander Hamilton later wrote, "everything that is amiable in virtue, in fortitude, in delicate sentiment and accomplished manners, pleads for him: but hard hearted policy calls for a sacrifice" (quoted in *Journal* 1904, p. 126).

Washington, who after all had the authority to sentence the prisoner on his own, had committed himself to follow the recommendation of the board; consequently, Major André, immediately after the tribunal's decision was rendered, was sentenced to be hanged. To the President of Congress General Washington reported:

> Sir,
>
> I have the honor to enclose Congress a copy of the proceedings of a board of General Officers in the case of Major André, Adjutant-General the British Army. This officer was executed, in pursuance of the Board, on Monday the 2nd instant, at twelve o'clock, at our late camp, at Tappan .... I have now the pleasure to communicate the names of the three persons who captured Major André, and who refused to release him, notwithstanding the most earnest importunities and assurances of a liberal reward on his part. Their names are, *John Paulding, David Williams,* and *Isaac Van Wert.* (*Andreana* 1865, pp. 5-6)

It remained for the Secretary of the Congress, Charles Thompson, to justify Washington's decision to the public. He drew particular notice to André's own evaluation that "I receive the greatest attention from his Excellency George Washington, and from every person under whose charge I have been placed" (Board of Inquiry Proceedings 1780, p. 21). Thompson, making the best possible case under the circumstances, reminded his readers of "the many other acknowledgments which he made of the good treatment he received," and that such admissions "must evince, that the proceedings against him were not guided by passion or resentment. The practice and usage of war were against his request, and made the indulgence he solicited, circumstanced as he was, inadmissible."

3

The Blackest Treason

Thompson told his readers that André's execution was carried out without "passion or resentment," but passion is exactly what the Arnold/André affair evoked among the revolutionists. In a letter to General Nathaniel Greene, Alexander Hamilton wrote (from Verplanck's Point, New York, September 25, 1780):

> Sir, There has just been unfolded at this place a scene of the blackest treason. Arnold has fled to the enemy. André the British Adjt Genl is in our possession as a spy. This capture unraveled the mystery. West Point was to have been the sacrifice, all the disposition have been made for the purpose and 'tis possible, tho' not probable tonight may still see the execution. The wind is fair, I came here in pursuit of Arnold but was too late I advise your putting the army under marching orders, and detaching a brigade immediately this way. I am with great regard/Your obedient servant/Alexn Hamilton/Aid de Camp.

The dates of these communications demonstrate how quickly the rebel army reacted. André was still imprisoned, letters and rumors implying negotiations to save him were flying around the colonies, and the Major's fate had yet to be decided. Almost immediately in a letter to Samuel Huntington, transmitting some of the same rhetoric (September 25, 1780) from Camp Tappan; in the Huntington Library's Greene papers collection), General Nathaniel Greene wrote,

> Sir, Enclosed I send your excellency a copy of a letter which this moment came to me from the hand of Col Hamilton communicating a discovery of the blackest treason that ever disgraced human nature. I have thought it advisable to forward your excellency this intelligence that you may take measures to search in his [Arnold's]

papers in Philadelphia, and those of his family with whom he is connected. Perhaps some discovery may be made which may lead to further scenes of villainy.

"The blackest treason that ever disgraced human nature" is not without passion. The times were not without passion; Arnold's intended treachery was not discovered without passion. In a letter to Washington from the encampment at Tappan on the same day (9/25/80) Greene wrote

> I beg leave to congratulate your excellency on the happy discovery [of the Arnold/André plot] but am struck with astonishment on the horrid reason. The plot being laid open I think the enemy will be altogether disconcerted for some days to come, and give you full time to make such dispositions for the better security of West Point as you may think necessary.

This is not the man that André might have chosen to conduct the Board of Inquiry regarding his alleged espionage. General Greene has already pronounced the act "the blackest treason" and expressed his astonishment at the horrid reason for it. In a civilian court, André's attorney would have disqualified Greene from serving on the jury.

Greene knew as well as anyone the inflammatory nature of the André execution. On the following day (10/3/80) he wrote to John Mathews from Camp Tappan, scene of the hanging: "but I am afraid they have furnished the enemy with some colourable pretense to treat [the American prisoners in Charlestown] with severity." He feared that these prisoners would

> meet with rigor by way of retaliation for the punishment inflicted upon Major Andree the British Adjutant General who was taken in the character of a spy and has suffered accordingly. The enemy among other measures taken for the saving of Andree mentioned the situation of your friends at Charlestown and avowed their intention to treat them in the same manner Andree suffered. And as he was a particular favorite of General Clinton I have much to apprehend from his temper and resentment .... I don't wonder that you write feelingly on the subject.

Greene acknowledged that this was one of those cases that justify the passions of the soul, and said of the Charlestown prisoners "he that can be a cold spectator to the sacrifice of his friends must be either wanting in friendship or insensible to the dictates of humanity." Greene vowed to do what he could to save the Charlestown prisoners "against any violence, but inclination without power avails but little." Greene concluded with the observation that "Arnold's late treason has filled us all with horror and astonishment" (letter of 10/8/80).

After André's capture and execution, the fear of spies was rampant among the colonials, so deeply had the Arnold/André affair jolted the confidence of the army. Spies were commonly used during the Revolution by both sides, but now the fact that they could be very dangerous people was highlighted. Greene wrote to Washington (10/8/80 from Verplanck's Point) that he had thought that the recent account given by an apprehended deserter "of sufficient importance to send an express; as the detection of spies is an interesting matter to the safety of an army and the more hazardous the business is rendered the more difficult it will be for the enemy to obtain intelligence." Five days later, Greene wrote to Washington that he had detached one hundred men to join the cavalry under Colonel Jameson "to cover the lower country," and Greene stated that he intended "to detach a party of fifty men more, on purpose to follow what are called the Cow-boys. This party I mean to be at liberty to pursue thieves through all their turnings and windings, as I am persuaded that 5000 men upon stationary guards would not prevent their inroads."

A sacrifice was demanded by the situation. Hamilton wrote that "Arnold or he must have been the victim," adding the obvious enthymeme that Arnold was out of their control. Washington commented that "the circumstances he was taken in justified it, and policy required a sacrifice" (Flexner 1953, p. 390). Then he added the sympathetic note that André "was more unfortunate than criminal." The treason, as we have seen, startled the colonists with doubt; civilians mistrusted the officers, the common soldiers their leaders, the more conservative officers were under suspicion everywhere. A failure to act decisively in the case would endanger the rebel cause; André had to die.

4
A Gentleman's Education

André's letter to Washington asking that he be shot like a gentleman rather than hanged like a common spy is in some ways the quintessence of his mature character. Though not "a gentleman born and bred," gentlemanliness was his ideal; it was an ethos expected of officers in His Majesty's service, and John André lived up to it more fully than most.

His background was international. His father was a Swiss merchant, his mother a Parisian visiting England (Flexner 1953, pp. 23-24). John was born (2 May 1750) in Genoa and raised in Geneva. He was the eldest, with a brother and three sisters. The family spent much time in England; and one of his biographers, Winthrop Sargent (*Life* 1902) claimed (though it is now questioned by others) that he was educated at St. Paul's, Westminster. Less controversially, he was formally educated at the Academy of Geneva (later to be the University of Geneva) and was remembered as "a delightful student" (Decker 1959, p. 30) who excelled in mathematics and military drawings. Languages—French, Italian, and German—came easily to him; other subjects—music, painting, and dancing—were de rigueur for Englishmen of culture. André was Henry Peacham's Compleat Gentleman. His preparations for an aristocratic life were for the first time interrupted, however, when his father called him home; the young student would have to give up his trivial pursuits and learn the serious business of accounting in the family business.

A hand-drawn map showing the rebel fortifications of Philadelphia, particularly those on Mud Island in the Delaware River, is now owned by the Huntington Library; it was drawn by André. It is one of more than forty military maps drawn by him and presented to Major General Charles Grey as part of his journal, a parting gift for the general when he returned to England (Lodge, 1903, p. 27). The cartographer's hand is a delicate one; details are carefully and elaborately—and attractively—sketched in. André was a good draftsman; the map shows attention to detail, is precise, and has even been executed with attention to aesthetics. The man who rendered it was interested in accuracy, but at the same time eager to create a pleasing object. The location of several gunboats in the harbor is precisely drawn, together with instructions on how to reduce them and to compromise the city. The smallest significant detail has been included: ships, guns, fortified points of land, impassable marshes. The draftsman has done a careful, professional job. He shows himself a painstaking, thoughtful man with a flair for rendering detailed abstractions with a pen. He is precise and, above all, clear; the map speaks highly of the discipline and thoughtfulness of its maker.

Then, in 1769, when John was twenty, his father died; he inherited a substantial sum—25,000 pounds to be divided among the five children when they reached maturity (Hatch 1986, p. 13). Mrs. André took John and his oldest sisters and soon moved temporarily to rural Buxton in Derbyshire, primarily a secluded vacation spot where they could get away from the unpleasant memories of his father's life.

There he met, and was taken into protective custody by, Anna Seward, a twenty-six-year-old poetess who was eventually to achieve considerable fame in England for her verses. Hatch characterizes her father as a "poet of local repute" (1986, p. 14). Samuel Johnson, who had studied with Anna's grandfather, thought that he had never taught a boy in his life: he whipped, "and they learned" (Hatch 1986, p. 18). As André was a young man of some charm, wit and imagination, Miss Seward may even have thought that he had some talent. She introduced him to her literary coterie. His poetry has been characterized by Decker as "silly verse" (p. 31).

During the next several months John André was constantly in the company of Honora Sneyd, one of the "group," an intimate companion of Anna's who had lived with the Sewards after her mother died; she and John became engaged, though she does not appear to have been wildly enthusiastic about him. He wrote some verse about his feelings, and painted her portrait in miniature; he kept the original and gave her a copy in a locket (Hatch 1986, pp. 15-18). Parents on both sides objected to the proposed match: they were both still very young, and most important to Ms. Sneyd's parents was the obvious fact that young John had yet to demonstrate an ability to earn money. Shortly thereafter he returned home to fulfill his obligations to the family business, though maintaining a correspondence with both Anna and Honora. Their communications lasted for more than a year, Anna responding faithfully, Honora less so; André illuminated his letters to her with his drawings. Eventually she broke the engagement—he didn't have "the reasoning mind she required" (Hatch 1986, p. 24)—and married another, Richard Lovell Edgeworth.

Shortly after (1771), André abandoned his brief life as a merchant and purchased a second lieutenant's commission in the 23rd Foot, the Royal Welsh Fusiliers. And a short while after that he advanced his military career a notch further when he purchased a first lieutenancy in the 7th foot.

His regiment was assigned to Quebec City, Canada, and he was ordered to join it there. Officers were permitted to travel to their foreign assignments at their own expense, the procedure André chose. His assignment to the colonies landed him first in Philadelphia in September of 1775, a city boiling over with revolutionary sentiment, as he was to learn from officers of the Royal Irish posted there. When he decided to ride to Canada to join his regiment, he chose an inland, "scenic" route, through the Lake Champlain and Lake George regions in present-day New York State.

His first combat assignment was at Fort St. Johns (Major Charles Preston commanding), quickly under siege by a combined force of Americans, sympathetic Canadians, and a few French Canadians and Indians. The fighting was light, almost casual, and at its most intense, sporadic. But gradually, relentlessly, eventually, the British garrison was reduced, by occasional sniper fire, by more occasionally lobbed mortar shells, by food shortages, and by the onset of winter (Hatch 1986, pp. 43-49). The fort surrendered in early November, 1776, and the members of the garrison were sent as prisoners of war to the colonies.

André's first experience of war was not what he had expected. In Philadelphia, then Boston, and finally Montreal (where he was assigned as a prisoner to see after his regiment's baggage), he saw the streets fill with the unruly, the frightened, the hungry, the cold, and threadbare. Angry colonists were everywhere, disobedient, defiant, truculent, in Boston even more than in Philadelphia. People wandered about aimlessly, frightened into a kind of stupor. Some, thinking that the end of their world was near, tried to sell their possessions, at whatever price they could get. It was a glimpse of the apocalypse, a moment's view of the end of the world. Everywhere disorder. Like many of his nation and class, he did not understand the rationale for the rebellion; it was much ado about relatively little. He did not understand why Englishmen would rebel against their King over such matters as the Stamp Tax or the Townshend Acts. Whatever his inclination toward the arts, to poetic expression, to the unfettered life of the spirit, he was politically a Tory, much a political creature of his time and class.

And he was very much the professional soldier now. As a prisoner he got to see the Continental Army up close, got to scrutinize and evaluate it at leisure and at length. He viewed the conquerors as ragged, undisciplined, badly trained, and flagrantly unprofessional soldiers. The American officers were little better than their men, it seemed to him. And as many a soldier before and after would do, he did not attribute the loss of Fort St. Johns to the enemy's superiority in any way, but to his own garrison's shortages of food and munitions (Hatch 1986, p. 51).

Thus, after just months with his regiment, he saw a bit of fighting but also witnessed the traumatic blows of war on noncombatants. His capture by the Americans barely changed the conclusions he may have drawn from his experiences; his life view was reinforced, not altered.

Life for a captive officer in a European war was hardly demeaning in the eighteenth century. At Albany, where he stayed for nearly a month collecting his regiment's baggage as it arrived haphazardly from Canada, he was the guest of the royal governor, where he was well fed and cosseted; some of his spare time was spent making drawings of the governor's household. So too at Haverstraw and at Philadelphia, where he continued his self-appointed role of *bon vivant* socialite, though still a prisoner of war. While in Philadelphia (en route to imprisonment in Lancaster, Pennsylvania), he sketched a cameo of Rebecca Franks (daughter of a wealthy merchant) and is said to have presented it to her along with some lines of his own verse; he was becoming practiced at courtly flattery. And he found time to flirt with the beautiful, moody fifteen-year-old Peggy Shippen (Flexner 1953, p. 139). In a few years she would become the wife of Benedict Arnold.

Her influential family gave their name to Shippensburg, Pennsylvania. In Lancaster, where many British prisoners of all ranks were incarcerated, officers paid for their own lodging and meals themselves; André ingratiated himself with German settlers in town (he knew their language and had traveled in their country) and with Loyalists. Since he was also a gentleman of obvious attainments, he was also accepted by the socially prominent in the town. André found comfortable and congenial shelter in the prosperous and well-tended home of Caleb Cope, a pacifist Quaker who was not bothered by André's reduced status. In return for his housing and meals, André performed (he was an amateur musician) and gave drawing lessons to his host's twelve-year-old son (Hatch 1968, pp. 58-60).

In Carlisle, Pennsylvania, where André was reassigned in March 1776, life was more challenging. The local Scotch-Irish residents, mainly farmers and frontiersmen, were overtly hostile to the captured British officers and gentlemen who deported themselves in town, resplendent in their tailored regimentals. Days there were charged with high tension. One time the house where André was lodged was fired on by an angry crowd which had heard the (false) rumor that its resident had, while in Canada, encouraged the mistreatment of American prisoners (Flexner 1953, p. 145). And André's elegant demeanor, sauntering as he often did with his two bird dogs (Decker 1959, p. 37), was especially provoking; citizens spat on him, and when his life was threatened he decided to remain continually in his quarters.

Lord Howe, meanwhile, was engaged in several battles in New Jersey, winning some and losing some; the rebels could not be fatally engaged, and nothing of serious consequence occurred on this campaign. He commanded an amphibious force which, after several harassing and extended missions of his own, sailed back to New York harbor in June; and during the next few months drove the rebels out of the city and nearby Long Island. An exchange of war prisoners was arranged, and André was one of the fortunate ones to be returned. He rejoined his King's army in New Brunswick, New Jersey, and when he was ordered to return home for recruitment duty, he bought a captaincy in the 26th.

He volunteered his services as a staff officer, particularly as an interpreter to the Hessian forces attached to the British army; he was one of the very few English officers who could speak to the Hessian mercenaries in their own language, and was sent to New York where he sought, and was granted, a staff assignment with British headquarters. Lodge (1903, p. 11) claims that Howe wanted to promote him because of his many talents. Later, in June 1777, André was made aide-de-camp to Major General Charles Grey (Hatch 1986, pp. 72-73). During that year he was present at Brandywine, Germantown, and the capture of Philadelphia (*Andreana* 1874, II:54).

At the very end of 1777 the British army took up winter quarters in Philadelphia, and André, as did everyone else, expected it to be a quiet time. Militarily it was; socially the winter months were quite active for André and his fellow officers; he had become a leading member of "Howe's Thespians." They produced theatricals to relieve their boredom, to show off their extra military accomplishments, for their own entertainment and that of the local colonists (Flexner 1953, pp. 202ff.) In costume, performing on the flute, reciting poetry (some of it his own), acting the delicate gallant to the most gracious and attractive of the Philadelphia smart set, André was at least as comfortable as he was as aide-de-camp in the field. This was his other life, his other world, and it is not always apparent which existence held primacy for him, so able and so enthusiastic was he in both spheres; when it came down to it, though, he knew what was the really serious business: in New York, instructing Joseph Stansbury on the method of the initial contact with Arnold (via Peggy by way of her friend, Peggy Chew), André remarked that the letters should seem innocuous and might talk of such things as the masked ball in Philadelphia "and other nonsense" (Flexner 1953, p. 280).

When Grey was reassigned after winning too vigorously at Paoli and again at Tappan (ordering bayonet charges that caught many of the Americans still in bed), and Howe was recalled to England, he took care of André, seeing him placed on the staff of Sir Henry Clinton, Howe's successor. André became, among his other duties, chief intelligence officer (Hatch 1986, pp. 120-21). The intelligence that André had earlier been able to gather about the rebel forces in New Jersey, observations that he was able to relay to the British staff as a result of his journey through that area, was on-the-job training for him. His reports to British headquarters showed that he had ability and a gift for intelligence work. Most valuably, he was able to provide maps of the area, drawn from his memory of the terrain. On Clinton's staff, André's first important assignment was as part of a two-man negotiating team to arrange for an exchange of prisoners; it came to nothing (Flexner 1953, pp. 270-71).

5

The Arnold Enlistment

Late in April 1779, as Clinton's intelligence officer, André was given charge of the delicate operation of recruiting or possibly turning known discontents among the rebels. No thought was initially given to colonial General of the Army Benedict Arnold. Fortuitously, serendipitously, on 10 May 1779 Joseph Stansbury and the Reverend Jonathan Odell came to André to tell him that Arnold had indicated to Stansbury his disgust over the break with England and had expressed the fervent desire to end the bloodshed by offering his services to the British. At a price.

The American felt that he had been shabbily treated by his commanders, was in desperate need of money, and had convinced himself (or was convinced by his young wife, Peggy) that various economic and political signs meant that the American experiment would shortly fail. André and Arnold had, at varying times, moved in the same social circles, and much has been made of the irony of the Englishman's brief flirtation with Peggy Shippen before she married Arnold; but the two men had never met, an especial complication in this instance because André could not rely implicitly on Arnold's word or his actions, and the American for his part was a kind of treasonous entrepreneur, reasonably enough suspicious of everyone, as he was about to begin bargaining with the enemy over the value of the intelligence he could send them.

André's duties as chief of intelligence operations did not take up all of his time. Nevertheless, his attempt during the initial stages of the Arnold "enlistment" was deft in conception—all the more striking in view of the operation's subsequent blunders—though nothing ever came of this first approach. In his initial communication with Arnold he chose a complicated subterfuge, showing that he was imaginative at planning intelligence operations, although his forte was not in the execution of them; he was not a field man. He wrote a letter to an acquaintance of his and a known confidante of Peggy Arnold, urging her to show it to the general's wife. In the reply, Mrs. Arnold would add her own message, between the lines, in invisible ink (Hatch 1986, p. 169).

This initial gambit ended in frustrated failure. The British, who had never imagined that Arnold might defect, recovered quickly, and André entered into correspondence with Peggy Shippen Arnold as described above. He wanted hard data about West Point; she sent him, along with useless low-grade material, shopping lists of wanted millinery merchandise which should be available in New York. In exasperation, André replied that His Majesty's coffers would not open a sliver until some important information was forthcoming—an accurate plan of the Point, details of the placement of American boats patrolling the Hudson, the order of battle of the American army. Almost contemptuously he urged her to overcome the general's lethargic inability to develop the information he wanted: "permit me to prescribe a little exertion" (Flexner 1953, pp. 289-91). Not the way a captain (André's rank at the moment) normally addressed the wife of a major general, particularly in so tender a situation. For whatever reason, the next missive from Mrs. Arnold broke off negotiations. The general would get his price, it said in coded phrases, one way or another. As we now know, the door was only temporarily closed.

The operation was certainly ludicrously inept by modern standards and practices. Part of that was due to the amateur status of the principals; skilled espionage agents were in scarce supply anywhere at that time, but especially in the Continental Army. The British had some trained agents of their own, and had success in employing indigenous Tories. Part of the ineptitude (on both sides) came about because much of the technology of espionage had not yet been developed—would not be for centuries—thus ruling out any degree of sophistication.

For instance, the chain of intelligence transmission involved at least two individuals who had to transmit information between the principals, and communications were often sent in the writer's hand. Arnold (who signed himself as "J. Moore," "A.G." or "Gustavus," but who could have been easily identified by the content of his letters) used as a contact Stansbury, who signed himself more conspicuously as "Jonathan Stevens." The contact on the British end was the Reverend Jonathan Odell, known as "J. Osborne." André was one of the least subtle of all: his code names were "John Anderson," "John Andrews," or "J.A." "Anderson" was his cover name when he was apprehended.

Jargon code has a dignified antiquity, having been used at least as early as Cicero's time; on the other hand, its effectiveness, according to David Kahn (1978, p. 290) caused it to be used by German agents as recently as 1940. And yet, seemingly obvious as were most of these names in the André/Arnold affair, they were adequate for the purpose, if we may judge anything from their not having been important legal elements at André's trial. They may not have needed computers to select code names at random; finally, it was not a deciphered code name that blew André's mission and his cover.

At one point the Reverend Odell became intrigued by a mark on a letter in his charge; and though the page was mainly blank, he was sure it contained a secret communication that he desired to know. What he saw was, in Hatch's words (1986, pp. 172-73), "a vast splotch." At some point in its provenance the page had gotten wet; Odell found that of the entire message "not the half of any one line can be made legible"; and then he added to its inscrutability by holding the page over a candle for so long that it was then impossible to refold it.

Invisible ink was occasionally used in the communications of the Arnold/André "network," a technology at least as old as Pliny the Elder (Kahn 1978, p. 290). The conspirators used codes "keyed to Bailey's *Dictionary* or Blackstone's *Commentaries*" (Hatch 1968, p. 169). "Keyed" meant that each word in a communication was identified by number (identifying page and line); such codes are very difficult to break without a computer, unless the decoder has the book being used as the key; variations of this code are still used for low-level communications today. Arnold and André sometimes wrote in a rhetoric supposed to be that of merchants engaged in normal business commerce. But each party was wary of the negotiations since they had never met or had other close contact. And Arnold was holding out for 10,000 pounds; André wanted to assure himself that the information—and the West Point plans—were worth the high asking price. That desire to meet, to get a chance to evaluate the other firsthand, was to be their undoing. That need to deal with the other principal face-to-face would bring André across rebel lines and into the neutral ground, where he would be vulnerable.

Arnold wrote a coded letter, "keyed to a small dictionary," addressed to "Mr. Anderson" on 15 July:

> On the 13th Instant I addressed a letter to you expressing my Sentiments and expectations, viz, that the following Preliminaries be settled previous to coöperating. First, that S. Henry secure to me my property, valued at ten thousand pounds Sterling, to be paid to me or my Heirs in case of Loss; and, as soon as that shall happen, _____ hundred pounds per annum to be secured to me for life, in lieu of the pay and emoluments I give up, for my Services as they shall deserve—If I point out a plan of coöperation by which S. H. shall possess himself of West point, the Garrison, &c. &c. &c. twenty thousand pounds Sterling I think will be a cheap purchase for an object of so much importance .... I expect a full and explicit answer. (Van Doren 1941, pp. 464-65)

Clinton was at the time busy with other military matters as well—preparing for an imagined French invasion of Rhode Island, for one—and did not pursue negotiations with Arnold full speed. Also, there was some lingering doubt about the American general; he constantly bickered with the Continental Congress, and a pending court-martial had left him a diminished hero. On 24 July Odell wrote to Stansbury in his own hand (André and Arnold were the terminals of the actual communications circuit), being unintentionally explicit enough (if the letter had gotten into unfriendly hands) to have Arnold hanged and the whole network blown and sentenced to a similar fate:

> His Excellency authorizes me to repeat in the strongest terms the assurances so often given to your Partner, that if he is in earnest and will to the extent of his Ability coöperate with us, he *shall* not in any possible event have cause to complain, and essential Services *shall* be even profusely rewarded, far beyond the stipulated indemnification (as a preliminary) is what Sir H. thinks highly unreasonable. However he has not the smallest doubt but that everything may be settled to mutual satisfaction when the projected interview takes place at W. P. from whence it is expected Mr. M will take occasion ... to correspond with S. H. by flag of truce. Mr. Anderson is willing himself to effect the meeting either in the way proposed or in whatever manner may at the time appear most eligible. (Van Doren 1941, pp. 465-66)

Arnold, assuming a seller's market, was demanding and insistent; he wanted 10,000 pounds for his services to the crown, and full reimbursement for any property that he might lose as a result of his loyalty (Hatch 1986, p. 177). Clinton, appreciating Arnold's need for cash, at that point took a contemplative step backward. André was instructed to reply evasively, and Arnold found the response so "laconic" that he thought about breaking off negotiations. But the haggling was merely a momentary glitch; Arnold was determined to peddle his information and the property at West Point, while the British were not willing to pay anything for less than services rendered—the principle of the bird in the hand, and so on. Yet despite André's laconic reserve, Arnold became more confident than ever that a deal could be struck.

Odell intervened, with a positive outcome for the conspiracy this time. Writing to André, he lamented a misunderstanding on the part of his "friend's friend" (Arnold), and urged the adjutant general "to write once more at least" (Hatch 1986, p. 178). Communications were reopened, and Arnold responded by sending some relatively innocuous intelligence; André thanked him, but pointed out that West Point was the target of prime concern.

Arnold, realizing that written communication had its limitations, wanted a face-to-face meeting with André. He could make his case for his reimbursement much more forcefully, no doubt, and argued with his British co-conspirator that he was "convinced a conversation of a few minutes would satisfy you entirely, and I trust would give us equal cause to be pleased" (Hatch 1986, p. 179). In some ways André was not so anxious for such a meeting: it would be on Arnold's turf and he was, after all, a very high-ranking officer in the British army, which could not afford to send such a valuable person on so dangerous a mission. No army could. Yet, with the war seemingly winding down to the crown's advantage, with the rebel government and army seeming to come apart at its seams, a Continental Army at Camden just recently devastated, the capture of West Point may well have seemed like a decisive blow—perhaps the decisive stroke—of the (soon to be ended) war. With so much at stake, André decided to forsake prudent discretion.

Meanwhile, he had a complicated spy apparatus to run. André was simultaneously directing the recruitment and interrogation of defectors, Loyalists living within American lines who knew something about Washington's forces, runaway slaves, returned and escaped prisoners of war. While negotiations with Arnold dragged on, he was learning a lot about West Point from various sources: a German prisoner of war, the wife of a British deserter, and by double agent Elijah Hunter. The capture of some of Major Benjamin Tallmadge's personal papers provided André with additional information. And British intelligence was running Ann Bates, one of the most successful spies of the war, one of the few women espionage agents of note of any time. She had been used on a variety of missions and gained recognition for her dependability and productivity. André used her in the initial stages of his contact with Arnold (she, in turn, was in touch with Arnold). An index of her resourcefulness is shown in the information she gathered about the Continentals' shipping and food supplies (Hatch 1986, pp. 183-84).

On 30 August Arnold wrote the now famous (infamous?) "Gustavus letter" to André, "in a disguised hand" (Van Doren 1941, p. 470). After excusing himself for not having written sooner, Arnold noted that in a very few days he expected to be able to "procure" an interview for André with himself (Mr. M, or M———e),

> when you will be able to settle your commercial plan I hope agreeable to all parties. Mr. M———e assures me that he is still of opinion that his first proposal is by no means unreasonable and makes no doubt when he has a conference with you that you will close with it. He expects when you meet that you will be fully authorised from your house: that the risques, and profit of the co-partnership may be fully and clearly understood .... Mr. M———e flatters himself that in the course of ten days he will have the pleasure of seeing you, He requests me to advise you that he has ordered a draught on you in favor of our mutual friend S [Stansbury] for £300—which you will charge on acct of the tobacco.

Had this sort of communication been sent in modern times, it would have aroused the suspicions of a contemporary censor, certainly if the writer or the addressee were under surveillance. In 1780, when it was written and received, no special notice was taken of it. Arnold had given it to William Heron, whom he trusted and who was on his way to New York. But Heron was a double agent in business-for-self, selling intelligence to both sides; he opened it and became suspicious when he saw that it had been signed in a disguised hand (Decker 1959, p. 53). Back in Redding, Connecticut—he did not deliver the letter when he was in New York—he gave it to a friend, General Samuel Parsons, to evaluate. Taking it at face value—a letter about mercantile affairs—Parsons consequently did nothing about it until Arnold's treachery was uncovered.

In early September André experienced a happy interruption in his dealings with the Arnold affair. Sir Henry Clinton's adjutant general and his deputy resigned their posts because of irreconcilable differences with their commander. Officers had those options in the eighteenth century. André, ever ambitious, and much in Sir Henry's favor, was offered the job. Actually, he was the second officer approached. He of course accepted. The matter was not so clear-cut as it would be today: the retiring adjutant general left to rejoin his old regiment, and André agreed to purchase his position for 300 pounds a year. And then André's rank was brevet major, the full status having to await approval of London (Hatch 1986, pp. 187-90). He did not have to wait long to have the brevet rank replaced by a regular appointment as adjutant general—the end of August of 1780.

On 11 September, Arnold and André had arranged to meet at Dobbs Ferry; the latter was accompanied by Colonel Beverly Robinson, a recent defector to the royalist cause, described by Hatch as a "seasoned Intelligence officer" (1986, p. 217). Clinton's idea was that Robinson would pretend to be negotiating for the release of some property confiscated after his defection, an errand he had conducted before. Supposedly, that would enable the accompanying André to meet with Arnold. But the plan was initially frustrated when a small gunboat from the British man-of-war *Vulture* fired on Arnold's barge, forcing its return to the far bank. Once separated, neither party would risk a meeting, and so the conference was put on hold. Each agent withdrew to safe ground.

On 15 September the impatient Arnold decided to make another attempt. Signing himself "Gustavus," he wrote a letter to Mr. John Anderson again, care of Mr. James Osborne, to be left at the Rev. Odell's in New York:

> If you think proper to pursue your Former Plan, you will be perfectly safe in Coming to his quarters or those of Major Tallmadge of his regiment either of those gentlemen will immediately send an Escort with you to meet me: If you have any objections to this plan, I will send a person in whom you may Confide, by Water to meet you at Dobb's Ferry on Wednesday the 20th Inst between 11 & 12 oClock at Night, who will Conduct you to a place of safety, where I will meet you. It will be necessary for you to be disguised, and if the Enemies Boats are there it will favor my Plan as the Person is not Suspected by them .... (Van Doren, *Secret History*)

And thus was André's fate offered to him.

On 16 September a second meeting was planned. HMS *Vulture* was ordered to proceed up the Hudson to Teller's Point, slightly north of today's Sing Sing. Colonel Robinson was on board, still using the ruse of trying to contact the American authorities about his confiscated property. André was to proceed upriver in a smaller craft and await the right minute to go ashore while aboard the *Vulture*. He set out from the British lines on 20 September. General Benedict Arnold was busy with his military duties, which now included entertaining his commander-in-chief, who was in the area, primarily to consult with his French allies.

The tradecraft of espionage was still in a very primitive state, hampered, as already noted, by an uncomplicated technology. Arnold and André were nevertheless, even within this context, clumsily inexpert and disorganized. André was sailed up the Hudson and placed on board the *Vulture*. Robinson and Captain Andrew Sutherland met him there, and they began their wait for the arrival of Arnold's contact, Joshua Smith (Hatch 1986, p. 225). Another glitch: Smith did not show up, but rather than cancel the operation, André decided to stay in place for another day. He sent an unsealed letter to Clinton complaining of a stomach disorder which would prevent his return, but in a sealed letter he confided to his commander that because he was cognizant of the dangers of attempting yet another separate encounter with Arnold, he had decided to remain on board the *Vulture* and to try one more time to meet with Arnold (Hatch 1986, pp. 225-26).

The American was unable to contact the *Vulture* on the night of the 20th, the agreed-upon rendezvous. The contact, Joshua Smith, had been unable to provide either the boat or the oarsmen which would have ferried André ashore. André, dressed in his bright red regimentals, white-topped boots, and billowing officer's cloak, did not want to miss yet another opportunity for an interview with Arnold, and decided to risk sending a letter—under flag of truce—to the general, but written in his own hand and signed "John Anderson" (Decker 1959, pp. 62-63). The purpose of this letter was simply to inform Arnold that he was still holding himself in readiness, awaiting the arranged interview.

Yet another glitch. Joshua Smith, acting as Arnold's agent, had been unable to get two tenants of his to row him to the British warship. Samuel Colquhoun—his name is almost always spelled "Cahoon," presumably because that is a close phonetic rendering of it—was tired and apprehensive. He had been up for most of the night, and the idea of rowing a longboat (or whaleboat?) was more than one man could handle; he was also wary of rowing near an armed enemy ship, just as wary of the response of American forces should he be seen approaching the enemy.

Arnold, like André, wanted badly to transact the proposed business. So the following night he set out for Smith's house himself. There he alternately cajoled, threatened, and appealed to the patriotism of Cahoon to ferry Smith out to the *Vulture*. Smith was undecided when his wife met him and advised strongly against the idea; he went back to Arnold and asked to be excused from this job, but the general warned him that if he failed in this, his patriotic duty, he would be reported as "a disaffected man" (Hatch 1986, p. 227). Samuel's brother, Joseph, was equally reluctant to row out on the river at night, but with a rhetorical combination of appeals to his patriotism and soothing assurances that all would go smoothly and uneventfully, Arnold finally persuaded both men to row Smith out on the river to the British warship.

Finally, late in the night of the 21st-22nd Joshua Smith boarded the *Vulture* to deliver a letter to "Mr. Robinson." The letter informed André that Smith, ignorant of what was developing, would conduct him to a safe and relatively private place. Accompanying the letter was a slip of paper written by Arnold, undisguised, from "Gustavus to John Anderson" (Decker 1959, p. 64). André made final preparations; he would travel to the western shore alone (Arnold's pass did not mention Beverly Robinson), and he insisted on wearing his British uniform. Clinton had demanded this, not that André needed pictures drawn on this account. And his commander also recalled after the episode's unhappy end that he had also insisted that André not use another name and not cross enemy lines. Sir Henry was uneasy about the danger inherent in the operation from the beginning; his own choice for the mission was to have been Beverly Robinson (Hatch 1986, pp. 224-25), but André's zeal prevailed, and he himself went.

Shortly after midnight on the night of the 21st-22nd, André got into the longboat and was rowed ashore to a point just below Haverstraw from where he journeyed north to find Arnold, finally meeting him around 2 a.m. They talked for too long a time; Arnold was insistent in his demands about payment, he said later, 20,000 pounds if he was able to provide West Point and 3,000 soldiers, 10,000 pounds regardless of the outcome (Hatch 1986, p. 231). Smith, waiting for them at the small wharf where they had docked their boat, after several hours went up to warn both men of the approaching dawn, urging them to hurry. The risk involved in returning to the *Vulture* when the river was lighted was incalculably greater. But the men nevertheless had more to discuss, the Cahoons were tired and dogged in their insistence that they not return to the *Vulture,* and André was persuaded, though much against his reasoned judgment, to further their discussions at "Belmont," Smith's house about four miles away.

André was now in deep. He had originally intended to return to the *Vulture* while it was still dark, but with approaching day he was urged to remain longer; that meant placing himself under Arnold's authority, and more important, it meant leaving a neutral area and passing through the lines of the Continental Army. He and Arnold were at one point stopped by sentries, but allowed to pass when Arnold was recognized. André, in defiance of Clinton's strong advice, had now been seen in Arnold's company. Early the next morning—22 September—they could hear cannon fire from downriver, and from Smith's house witnessed the *Vulture* withdrawing downstream under American fire. André was understandably "vexed" (Smith's description, Decker 1959, p. 66). The retreat of the *Vulture* meant that an alternative route of escape would have to be sought, and that route would have to be through country that André did not know, having to rely on a co-conspirator of dubious loyalties and judgment, having to pass through American lines and encountering their guards at unpredictable points and times, and running the gauntlet of all of the dangers and hidden vicissitudes of the neutral ground. Had the land mine been invented, André could be said to have been about to walk through a field thickly laden with them.

But he had little choice; and amateurish at covert behavior as he was, he did not have any alternative plans. Meanwhile Arnold gave him several sketches of the West Point fortifications and lists of its armaments, their placement, and so on. He suggested that André conceal these documents in his stockings (André later insisted), and the adjutant general reluctantly consented. Their discussions over later that day, Arnold wrote out yet three more passes: two to Smith, permitting passage by either land or water, and the other to André, permitting "John Anderson," who was on "public business," to travel to White Plains or below. The stipulation "or below" was intended to allow André to cross through the neutral ground (Decker 1959, p. 67).

West Point was to be compromised five days thereafter. Arnold had given André an accounting of the weak places in West Point's fortifications and the best ways of reducing them, estimates of troop strength, and as a bonus, a list of spies and informants operating in the area (Hatch 1986, p. 234); and if the British were lucky, they might also bag General Washington, who was in the region and whose precise whereabouts Arnold would signal to the invading British army when he knew them.

Arnold rode back to his headquarters late in the afternoon of the 22nd, leaving the responsibility of returning André to British lines in the hands of his accomplice, Joshua Smith. That cautious man, not wanting to be seen in the company of a uniformed British officer—he was already under suspicion in the neighborhood for alleged Tory sympathies—felt that the *Vulture* was now too far downstream to permit safe reboarding, and began making other plans. André was now extremely vulnerable; unexpected circumstances, his own lack of preparation, and his willingness to go along with Arnold's hazardous suggestions engulfed him in danger. It was a peril which events had established, further enhanced by the incompetence (and lack of serious concern for his welfare) of his American co-conspirators. But it was a peril he lacked the skill, inclination, and ability to avoid. Thus, when Smith urged him to doff his regimentals and put on a dark crimson cloak and beaver hat, André complied. Now his peril was mortal: he was out of uniform, in civilian attire, in enemy territory.

About the time that Arnold was returning to the safety of his headquarters, the disguised André, Smith, and a servant rode on the track toward (the now desolate) King's Ferry. They crossed to the east bank of the Hudson at Verplanck's Point without incident. East of Peekskill they were challenged by Continentals, who warned them of the danger of passing through the neutral ground at night, especially since the immediate area had recently been harassed by marauding Cow-boys. André wanted to press ahead—probably foolishly—but Smith convinced him that they would be better off at the nearby house of friendly Andreas Miller (Decker 1959, p. 69).

Early on the morning of 23 September, a Saturday, Major—now citizen—André was anxious to get under way. Joshua Smith, who had less at stake, was less impatient. When they did take to the road, their pace was deliberate. A picket stopped them near Crompond Corner, the most modest of settlements, but waved them on after his superior officer, a Captain Ebenezer Foote, approved the pass from Arnold. Smith bought them breakfast at the home of a Mrs. Underhill, a meager meal of mush and milk. Here Smith decided on, and announced to André, his intention to leave him, though originally his intention was to escort his charge all the way to White Plains, still fifteen miles farther ahead. The British officer was now to be entirely on his own; he had reached that unhappy state through a series of events over which he could not exert influence. Smith's decision to abandon him was the final link in an interlocking, interrelated chain. When they parted, Smith gave him forty Continental dollars to get him "home" (Decker 1959, p. 71). André was now alone in the neutral ground, said to be active with guerrilla forces, out of uniform yet clearly not a citizen of the region—he would have to ask directions of several people along the way. And he had concealed in his British army boots papers whose revelation would mean his death.

André made his way toward Tarrytown, alternately riding and stopping to ask directions. He is known to have asked the way of Stevenson Thorne, and from Staats Hammond at Pleasantville to have learned of active parties of rebel scouts operating around Young's Tavern to the south of his position. At a fork in the road known as Mekeel's Corners, finding that Whig soldiers were at Young's Corners to the southeast, he doubled back for a mile or so and then descended a path leading directly to Tarrytown. At about nine-thirty that morning André stopped again, to study a map.

6

This Is a Spy!

Now it happened that André's worst-case scenario would be realized. The road he traveled was patrolled by several irregulars: seven in number, they were former militiamen out to perform a little ad hoc patriotism. Apologists have described them as patriots defending the area from Cow-boys; others have claimed that they were going to stop any likely traveler who came in sight, and liberate him of his property (Decker 1959, p. 74). André was just such a victim. He had the bearing of a gentleman, was wearing white-topped boots, and was riding a valuable horse. While Isaac Van Wart and David Williams remained off to the side of the road, John Paulding stepped into the middle of it, leveling his musket at the stranger.

Once again, and most ineptly, André proved himself unable to cope with the ordinary demands placed on spies. When Paulding asked him where he was going, André (according to Paulding; Hatch [p. 242] thought his testimony the most responsible) responded with, "My lads, I hope you belong to our party." This was really a reckless comment considering his situation, probably made because from the first André assumed that his assailants were Cow-boys loyal to the crown; it was reckless because he had no idea who had stopped him, particularly so since all he had to do was produce Arnold's pass entitling him to go to White Plains. When Paulding rejoined by asking him what "party" that was, André put his own head in a noose: "The lower."

James Fenimore Cooper's *Notions of the Americans* summarizes (and evaluates) the situation this way. "As there was nothing immediately in view about the person of Major

André to betray his real character, it is quite possible that, had he retained his presence of mind, he might, after a short detention, have been permitted to pass" (1828 I:280).

André was apprehended—it is of the greatest importance to note—not behind enemy (American) lines, but in that region between the lines—No-Man's-Land, the neutral ground. He was out of uniform, of course, but was that of itself criminal?

Cooper is more generous about the status of the arresting soldiers than have been others in the wake of Major Tallmadge's negative estimation. When a representative to Congress, Tallmadge spoke against the petition of these three men for an increase in pension. They had not arrested André out of patriotism, he insisted, "but in the hope of gain" *(The National Intelligencer,* 4 March 1817). Cooper credits their "sagacity" and describes them as "three young American farmers" lying in ambush "to await the passage of any small party of the British ... who might chance to come that way" (p. 280). The sagacious young men were immediately suspicious.

André then produced a gold watch—English officers were thought always to carry them—and claiming to be "an officer in the British service," he fatally announced, "on particular business in the country," and he urged them to let him pass. But the guerrillas had seen more than enough to satisfy their needs; they bad him dismount. He shortly produced the pass, so late probably because he was very nervous and fearful and not thinking efficiently. Van Wart came directly to the point. "Damn the pass!" (related in Decker 1959, p. 77)—and demanded to have André's money, since he had already claimed to be a British officer. They decided to search André immediately, having more than enough reason to believe that they had come across a lucrative catch, or more accurately, that a lucrative catch had come across them. They took him behind a fence running parallel to the road, and into the thicket just beyond, where André was forced to undress as each of his garments was searched.

At the last instant, when it looked as though André might elude capture this one more time and effect this closest of narrow escapes, David Williams got the idea to have their captive take off his boots. And there, at the bottom of his stocking, were some papers. Paulding—described as the most literate of the trio, but more likely the only one of them who could read—examined André's papers, recognized their significance, and exclaimed, "This is a spy!" (Hatch 1986, p. 244). Now it occurred to at least one of them, but probably all three, that they had cornered a fatter cat than they had earlier imagined. They asked André whether he would give them a hundred guineas and his horse and watch if they released him. He answered in the affirmative; but for some reason their patriotic fervor overcame them and they decided to turn this seemingly well-heeled gentleman over to the proper authorities. Williams subsequently testified that he denounced André's offer of gold in resounding rhetoric worthy of Cooper's most eloquent moments: "No, by God, if you give us 10,000 guineas, you should not stir a step" (Decker 1959, p. 78).

The status and intentions of these three irregulars is still unclear. To the emerging nation at the moment of André's capture they were heroes, and Washington treated them as such. But Lieutenant Joshua King, André's personal guard, and intelligence officer Tallmadge thought otherwise. Both of those officers felt that the three captors were Skinners, or highwaymen, in business for themselves, and that business was highway robbery. Tallmadge thought that as privateers of the neutral ground they were as liable to arrest as was André, so unsavory were the denizens of that liminal land. The area was as Cooper has described it, and the suspicion that the upstanding characters in *The Spy* had for Harvey Birch was the suspicion of Tallmadge for Paulding, Van Wart, and Williams. However, the overriding consideration seems to have been the capture of the second most important officer of the enemy army, and the thwarting of a potentially ruinous plot, one involving treason in high places. Under these circumstances, it was almost necessary to shower the three with praise and glory. Any other treatment of them would have seemed bizarrely inconsistent and suspicious to the public.

André was alert to what he perceived to be their avarice, and began to negotiate with them. He bargained with them, saying that if they took him to Kingsbridge (just north of what was then New York City), they would be handsomely rewarded, but they anticipated the possibility of their arrest there, with no reward at all. André then tried to reassure them by suggesting that one of them proceed to the British lines and pick up the ransom there. Decker remarks (1959, p. 78) that this proposal was tempting, and that the Americans deliberated at some length about it, but finally their fear of getting caught aiding the enemy for a bribe, however handsome, was too much for them.

They asked him where he had gotten the papers they had found on him, and again André's ineptness was apparent: "of a man in Pine's Bridge, a stranger to me" (Decker 1959, p. 79). Not even these unsophisticates were fooled by that ridiculous lie, and they decided to hand him over to regular army personnel. The nearest post known to them was in the John Robbins house in Kensico, and they set out in that direction, stopping a few times for food. At their objective they learned that a Lieutenant Colonel Jameson had moved his headquarters to North Castle, six miles farther (they had at that point already traveled six miles).

Colonel Jameson was understandably puzzled by the arrival of the irregulars and their prisoner. "John Anderson" had, on the one hand, a pass signed by General Arnold. It had granted him permission "to pass the guards to the White Plains or below if he chooses, he being on public business by my direction" (Hatch 1986, p. 3). But the stranger had been apprehended traveling south, and an earlier advisory delivered to Jameson alerted him to expect that a "John Anderson" would pass through the American lines heading north. More revealing were the documents, in Arnold's hand, pertaining to sensitive intelligence about the American stronghold at West Point.

Jameson decided to cover all possibilities: he dispatched Anderson under guard to Arnold's headquarters at the Robinson house. "Dispatch" is something of a euphemism here, since Anderson/André's arms were tied behind him, though he was mounted. But he also dispatched Captain Hoogland with the Arnold/West Point maps and lists to Washington, known to be returning from Hartford. Jameson was somewhat suspicious, but still uncertain of the potential explosiveness of the papers that had fallen into his hands. When Major Tallmadge returned to headquarters, he and

Jameson put their heads together: they were beginning to become suspicious of Arnold, but decided that if they failed to notify him of the capture of "Anderson" and his dangerous papers, they would be insubordinate—and they weren't willing to risk that (Flexner 1953, p. 361). So, along with the detachment escorting André, Jameson sent a note to Arnold, telling him that the retrieved papers, of "a very dangerous tendency" (Hatch 1986, p. 4), had been forwarded to General Washington. If Arnold could not have surmised the worst on seeing André being brought under guard toward him, he had the necessary details in Colonel Jameson's own words.

Unknown to the participants, Arnold, André, Jameson, and Washington, a race was on, the prize of which was to be survival for André, the loss of which would mean death. Arnold's life depended on his grasping the fundamentals of the rapidly changing situation before Washington was given the treasonous papers. If Jameson's intentions were to be fulfilled, and Anderson/André delivered to Arnold before any of the other details of the plot were revealed, the Englishman would be saved. Into this muddle, in which chance would have played so large a role, a new character entered, Major Benjamin Tallmadge, an intelligence officer newly returned from a mission near New York. Jameson was his superior and his senior, but Tallmadge, who could smell espionage and treason when it smashed him in the face, now had his suspicions thoroughly aroused. As the young major later testified, he had proposed alternative action, "offering to take the whole responsibility upon myself," but this was action that Jameson "deemed too perilous to permit" (Hatch 1986, p. 5). Tallmadge convinced the colonel to have André returned to their post at once. Tallmadge also tried to have the letter to Arnold recalled, but the colonel demurred at that idea. Inexplicably—or so it seemed to Tallmadge, then and ever after—Jameson insisted on letting the letter to Arnold get through unhindered (Hatch 1986, p. 5).

The messenger reached the party escorting Anderson/André, and brought him back to the Sand's Mills headquarters. But the letter to Arnold went back with the guard detail, and at Sand's Mills the courier carrying it was not intercepted, and he now set out again for the general.

Lieutenant Hoogland, sent to locate General Washington and to give him the Arnold/West Point papers, could not find him, and he returned to South Salem. Jameson and Tallmadge did not know what to do with Anderson/André now that he had been brought back to them, so they sent him on under guard to Colonel Elisha Sheldon's headquarters at South Salem, where he was placed under the immediate command of Lieutenant Joshua King. While there, André learned that the secret documents were to have been delivered to Washington and, now fully appreciative of the extent of his vulnerability, correctly identified himself to the lieutenant. King later recalled that although his captive was shabbily dressed and in need of a shave, when he saw the powder in his hair, he realized that the man was "no ordinary person" (Sargent 1904, p. 323). Tallmadge wrote that he suspected "John Anderson" right away when he noticed his "gait," that of a man "bred to arms" (Hatch 1986, p. 6). André, perhaps in an attempt to mitigate his offense in his captors' minds, now set about shedding light where he could, though that light would eventually mean his death.

That Sunday afternoon, telling his personal guard, Lieutenant King, that he "must make a confidant of somebody," he asked permission to write to Washington, identifying himself as "Major John André, adjutant general to the British Army" (Hatch 1986, pp. 6-7); "It is to vindicate my fame that I speak, and not to solicit security." Then he related the circumstances leading to his present incarceration. "I came up in the *Vulture* man-of-war for this effect."

Jameson's letter telling of the apprehension of a Mr. John Anderson and the documents he was carrying arrived at Arnold's headquarters first. He was at that moment playing the expectant host, with George Washington as his intended guest. Arnold rushed upstairs, had a brief conversation with his wife, and then rushed down again—"hobbled" is usually the way his movement is described—left word for General Washington that he had been summoned to West Point for a brief spell, and rode off to freedom.

Washington was kept busy by Arnold's assistant, John Lamb, who conducted a tour of the local defenses. When they returned to Arnold's headquarters, they found that their host had still not returned, but that Alexander Hamilton, Washington's aide, had just seen the incriminating papers and was beside himself. He also had possession of Jameson's letter and André's confession, all of which he shared with his commander immediately. Washington is said to have remarked some time later, "Whom can we trust now?" (Decker 1959, p. 94).

Hamilton and Washington had to act quickly, and they rapidly issued orders. A small detachment was sent to try to intercept Arnold, small because both men realized that he had probably already made good his escape. General Nathaniel Greene, commanding his unit in New Jersey, was ordered to march north with a brigade immediately. A letter from Arnold to his wife was given to her unopened: not even espionage and treason could cause a gentleman to violate his code of honor. Another, to Washington, was, of course, read by the general at once. Colonel Nathaniel Wade of Massachusetts was immediately appointed to command West Point. In the meantime, Washington reinforced the Point and surrounding posts. Joshua Smith was brusquely roused from his bed by armed troops, and marched off to be interrogated by Washington.

Washington also sent an order for Major André's guard to be alerted to the possibility of an attempted escape or rescue by British raiders, Colonel Jameson to assign as many men as possible to ensure the British officer's secure imprisonment. And to remove the prisoner from the proximity of the neutral ground, Washington ordered him brought north by some inconspicuous route. He added that he "would not wish André treated with insult; but he does not appear to stand upon the footing of a common prisoner of war ... and [he] is to be most closely and narrowly watched" (Decker 1959, p. 97).

Meanwhile, André was rapidly earning the friendship and respect of those he met—the gentlemen, anyway. Under the cognizance of Lieutenant King, he was quartered in the residence of Squire John Gilbert, specifically in the bedroom of Dr. Isaac Bronson. The adjutant general and the surgeon's mate took to each other at once; from Bronson we have learned that André felt certain that he would have been let go by these three men had he offered them "a single guinea." When André was taken away, Bronson told him that "whatever might be in his future destiny, he would never meet them hereafter as enemies."

Lieutenant King liked André from the first, and his counterpart in the Continental Army, Major Tallmadge, harbored negative feelings about neutral ground warriors. About André he wrote, in private correspondence, that though he might be the "greatest rogue that we have ever taken ... [he was] a very genteel, sensible man .... I wish he had been about a more honourable employment." Later, just before the execution, Tallmadge confided in a letter to a friend (*Andreana* 1865, p. 65) that André

> has unbosomed his heart to me so fully, and indeed let me know almost every motive of his actions since he came out on his last mission ... he has endeared me to him exceedingly. Unfortunate man! ... I am sure he will go to the gallows less fearful for his fate, and with less concern than I shall behold the tragedy. Had he been tried by a court of ladies, he is so genteel, handsome, polite a young gentleman, that I am confident they would have acquitted him.

After his hearing by the Board of General Officers, Alexander Hamilton wrote to his fiancée that "I wished myself possessed of André's accomplishments for your sake, for I would wish to charm you in every sense" (Hatch 1986, pp. 248-53, 267).

André's deportment and his letters following his capture would not win him his release on any grounds, but they would contribute to the durability of his legend. He is said to have told Hamilton that

> Sir Henry Clinton has been too good to me—he has been lavish of his kindness. I am bound to him by too many obligations and love him too well to bear the thought that he should reproach himself, or that others should reproach him, on the supposition of my having conceived myself obliged by his instructions to run the risk I did. I would not for the world leave a sting in his mind that should embitter his future days.

And to Sir Henry he wrote that he wanted "to remove from your breast any suspicion that I could imagine that I was bound by your excellency's orders to expose myself to what has happened" (Hatch 1986, pp. 267-68). And finally, he expressed solicitude for his mother and sisters, and requested that they receive any money due him after his (expected) execution.

Then during the following hours and days, Washington was besieged by correspondence from Colonel Beverly Robinson, Sir Henry Clinton, even Arnold himself, all on André's behalf. Robinson claimed that André was "on public business" and that "under these circumstances ... cannot be detained by you without the greatest violation of flags, and contrary to the custom and usage of all nations." Clinton's letter arrived on 26 September, arguing that André had proceeded beyond Continental lines at Arnold's bidding and request (certainly not an argument which the Americans would view with compassion), that he traveled under a flag of truce, and that passports were issued for his safe return. Arnold's letter arrived some days later, on 1 October. It repeated the points about André's traveling at Arnold's request, the flag of truce, the safe passport, the fact that he came ashore in full uniform (which he only changed at Arnold's "particular and pressing instance," and argued that the mission's purpose was "to carry letters, and for other purposes not mentioned." Then Arnold brought out his heavy weapons (though Flexner believes it to have been at Clinton's request [1975, pp. 388-89]): if Major André were to suffer, Arnold would seek bloody vengeance on those colonials then held captive in South Carolina, which would "in all probability open a scene of blood at which humanity will revolt" (Decker 1959, pp. 112-13).

General James Robertson also was not above the suggestion of such measures to Washington, but his expression of the idea lacked Arnold's bluntness. He reminded the American Commander-in-Chief that while the British had never put anyone to death for a breach of the rules of warfare (conveniently overlooking Nathan Hale), they had in their possession several such potential victims. If André were released, Robertson vowed, the British would release "any person you would please to name" in exchange (Hatch 1986, p. 265).

The letters punctuated more active attempts to free major André. There were negotiations, delegations, personal emissaries. But the position of Washington, and thus of the incipient republican officialdom, was firm. André had been captured out of uniform, behind enemy lines in time of war, on a clandestine mission whose purpose involved the defection of an American general and the compromise of his command. The major had been brought before a Board of General Officers which found him guilty of spying and which had recommended capital punishment, according to the usages of nations. Washington concurred with their findings and consequently ordered André's execution.

A delegation of Tory statesmen, including General Robertson, Lieutenant Governor Andrew Elliott, and Chief Justice William Smith (Joshua's brother), met with General Nathaniel Greene, who had chaired André's board, to plead for his release. Greene was equally firm: "... the case of an acknowledged spy admits of no discussion" (Decker 1959, p. 111). Greene is alleged to have said that Arnold was a rascal, but that André was "a man of honor whom he believed." Further trades were hinted at: André's safety for the return of Arnold. The British could not afford to be interested. Greene reported the British proposals to Washington, but had to report back to his counterparts that nothing made any "alteration in his opinion and determination." The matter was irreversibly settled; André's martyrdom was secure.

Weeping was said to have been common at the major's execution. Flexner points out (1953, p. 383) that André deported himself throughout his capture with "grace and fortitude"; he became, Flexner further argued, a symbol of the civilization which he had sought to preserve. American soldiers may have wept for the symbol they were destroying in the name of the brighter image they were now serving. We weep only for what we have lost, Father Ong once remarked to me.

7

Posthumous Encomia

And then the post-mortem rituals began. By 1821 the story of André's capture and execution had become something of an American folk epic (Pickering's Introduction to the 1971 edition of *The Spy*, p. 22). Cooper wrote about it in his 1828 *Notions of the Americans*. The British and the Tories and those who thought like them were outraged; the wrong villain had lived, and Washington had condemned to death the one noble man in the whole business. Americans agreed for the most part; the scoundrel in the affair had escaped, and André, noble and manly, had paid with his life. An illustrated broadside of 1780 depicts "A REPRESENTATION of the FIGURES exhibited and paraded through the Streets of Philadelphia, on Saturday, the 30*th* of *September*, 1780." A two-faced Arnold rides in a cart towards a large fire, a dark Satanic figure threatening him with a pitchfork. The text exults that the "Omniscient Creator ... has thrown into our hands ANDRE": and then as a contrast, for this little drama needs some noble figure to offset the infamous traitor: "ANDRE was gen'rous, true, and brave." The actual character of each actor was little known, and the artist/publisher (and almost immediately the public) created dramatic contrasts for themselves.

Arnold free and André hanged: it was one of the great ironies of the war. Yet, as later expressed by Cooper, most patriots felt that the results were lawful and necessary. The knowledgeable may have mourned the necessity of the execution, but did not flinch in their support of Washington's decision. He had correctly done his duty in support of the Republic; and André had done nothing to justify escaping from this lawfully inflicted fate.

Alexander Hamilton said of his former foe,

> There was something singularly interesting in the character and fortunes of André. To an excellent understanding, well improved by education and travel, he united a peculiar elegance of mind and manners, and the advantages of a pleasing person .... His knowledge appeared without ostentation, and embellished by a diffidence that rarely accompanies so many talents and accomplishments, which left you to suppose more than appeared. His eloqution was handsome; his address easy, polite and insinuating. (Flexner 1953, p. 383)

By either side, he was remembered. Cooper was one of those who remembered; as he wrote (and is quoted elsewhere in this book), André's death was a matter of the greatest solicitude with both armies. But more than that.

N. P. Willis wrote a poem *(Andreana* 1865, p. 51) which paraphrased André's letter to Washington; only the first stanza is quoted here:

> It is not the fear of death
>
> That damps my brow—
>
> It is not for another breath
>
> I ask thee now:
>
> I can die with a lip unstirred
>
> And a quiet heart,
>
> Let but the prayer be heard
>
> Ere I depart.

Anna Seward wrote quite a long poem, the *Monody* (more than thirty pages in print; in *Andreana* 1874, Huntington Library #1378, II:1 ff.), canonizing her friend and excoriating "Remorseless Washington." She vowed that he would one day repent "this barb'rous doom," and that the memory of "injured" André would arouse a vengeful army with "resistless fire." Washington's "guilt upbraided soul" would wish that "the sacred life" had never been stolen (Tillotson 1948, p. 186). Seward knew little of André's life in the colonies or the circumstances of his capture; but she did know the poetic structures of heroism. She imagines her hero at the forefront of an advancing army:

> Foremost in all the horrors of the day,
>
> Impetuous André leads the glorious way;
>
> Till, rashly bold, by numbers forc'd to yield,
>
> They drag him captive from the long-fought field.—
>
> Around the hero crowd th' exulting bands,
>
> And seize the spoils of war with bloody hands;
>
> Snatch the dark plumage from his awful crest,
>
> And tear the golden crescent from his breast;

Reckless of danger, André leads his badly outnumbered men in a glorious charge in which he, with great honor, is taken captive by savage hands. It is the old, traditional story of military heroism—the epic of defeat (see Rosenberg 1974). Washington, who might have spared him once he had been taken captive, is not spared by the poet:

> O Washington! I thought thee great and good,
>
> Nor knew thy Nero-thirst for guitless blood!
>
> Severe to use the pow'r that Fortune gave,
>
> Thou cool determin'd murderer of the brave!
>
> O dark and pitiless! your impious hate
>
> O'er-whelmed the hero in the ruffian's fate!

Personally, Washington considered André "a gallant and accomplished officer" (Flexner 1953, p. 383).

How enduring was the memory of the major's fate? In the War of 1812 no instance is recorded of attacking English soldiers crying out, "Remember André." The memory of the hanging does not seem to have been long, nor were its effects without future hope; John Puddicombe wished that this cruel barbarity might lead, by some unspecified path, to reconciliation:

> Return, though hapless, alienated child,
>
> To thy deserted parent! Oh! return,

> Deluded wanderer, to th' extended arms
> Of that indulgent Sovereign, whose commands
> Thou wast of old ambitious to obey! *(British Hero,* p. 22)

The response to André's fate was along national/political lines. Americans, we have seen, justified the hanging as an appropriate fate for a spy. Outraged and frightened by Arnold's treachery, the new republic's leaders demanded a sacrifice of their captive. The Americans were determined to assert the dignity of their new government. "The question was not one of vengeance" but of "more lofty considerations of sovereignty" (Cooper, *Notions,* I:292). But not all Americans felt that way. Cooper, in a letter to Thomas James De Lancey, observed from England that the sculpted heads of Washington and others had been defaced on André's monument: "You have heard," he wrote, "that the heads of Washington and the other American officers, which are on a bas-relief of André's monument, have been knocked off. This fact of itself furnishes proof of the state of feeling here, as respects us." *(Gleanings* 1982 rpt. p. 26.) A British custodial attendant blamed the vandalism on some "evil-disposed" American.

The British wrote that André's ineptness at espionage was a mark in his favor (Arnold, *New and Impartial Universal History,* p. 251). Charles Arnold is typical in this respect: André's "openness of behavior" merely saved the Americans the trouble "of producing so much evidence against him, as would otherwise have been indispensibly necessary to convict him" (Arnold, p. 251). And the British were quite angry about Washington, first for refusing to return the major's remains, and then for not affording him a burial with military honors. It was a "disgrace" to Washington's humanity (Arnold, p. 253).

The co-conspirators Arnold and André would always be remembered together, appropriately since they were both inextricably involved in the same plot. But for Americans as well as the British, they were decidedly different personalities, with markedly different characters. The remembrance of each would also be related to the other: as André was brave, noble, and unfortunate—the three epithets most commonly used to describe him—so Arnold was deceitful and treacherous. No matter whose version of this drama one heard (or read), the moral stature of Arnold and André varied little. The British were more indulgent of Arnold, of course, but he nevertheless was a traitor, and no one, even the beneficiaries of the committed treason, is greatly tolerant of such people. André was adored and admired by countrymen and foe alike, as Arnold was despised. "A London newspaper of 1782" printed the following acrostic on Arnold's name *(Andreana* 1865, p 57):

> Born for a curse to nature and mankind,
>
> Earth's broadest realms can't show so black a mind;
>
> Night's sable veil your crimes can never hide,
>
> Each one so great would glut historic tide;
>
> Defunct, your cursed memory will live
>
> In all the glare that infamy can give;
>
> Curses of ages will attend your name;
>
> Traitors will glory in your shame.
>
> Almighty vengeance earnestly waits to roll
>
> Rivers of sulphur on your treacherous soul;
>
> Nature looks down, with conscious error sad,
>
> On such a tarnished blot as she has made;
>
> Let hell receive you, rivetted in chains,
>
> Doomed to the hottest of its flames. (signed, AMERICAN)

These laureates were by no means alone in these adulatory expressions. Engravings and etchings of André appeared everywhere in English and American publications; occasionally one of Arnold too. For the most part they were busts of the British major, showing him even more boyishly handsome that he actually was. Occasionally depictions of his capture were attempted, and less frequently his hanging. These last were usually woodcuts. A great many of these works were executed during the century following André's execution, testifying to his popularity and his fame and stature as a hero and model of bravery. The Huntington Library alone has more than one hundred of these illustrations; and while a number of them are repetitions (six engravings by Rosenthal, for instance, from an original by Dodd; André's pen-and-ink self portrait inspired dozens more: Hall did more than a dozen himself, Jackman as least four, Pelton, Sherwin, and Hopwood several each), they were used separately to adorn different books. The sheer number of times that the major's likeness was used, and events from the life depicted, is cogent testimony to André's enduring fame and reputation.

Less than two decades after André's execution, William Dunlap wrote a play about his last days—*André: A Tragedy in Five Acts*—and produced it at the Park Theater in New York. It ran for one evening only, although it was revived twice more (for single performances) that same year. In his preface, Dunlap comments that he had chosen Major André as a subject nine years before (1790) but felt that recent events were not fit subjects for tragedy; on the other hand he did not want to fail to dramatize a story "so eminently fitted ... to excite interests in the breasts of an American audience" (1799, p. v). He knew that the details of the affair were fresh in the minds of his audience. All who knew André were his friends, "his misconduct [that of] submitting to be an instrument in a transaction of treachery and deceit" (1799, p. iv). Dunlap summarizes that veterans "must remember the diversity of opinion which agitated the minds of men at that time, on the question of the propriety of putting *André* to death" (1799, pp. iv-v).

The Prologue concludes with a pentameter poem (1799, p. viii):

> Who has forgot when gallant ANDRE dy'd?
>
> A name by Fate to Sorrow's self ally'd.
>
> Who has forgot when, o'er th' untimely bier,
>
> Contending armies paus'd—to drop a tear!

In the first act MELVILLE (inadvertently appropriate American literary name) praises the unfortunate André to his companion:

> The brave young man, who this day dies, was seiz'd
>
> Within our bounds, in rustic garb disguis'd.
>
> Yet not a heart but pities and would save him;

> For all confirm that his is brave and virtuous;
>
> Known, but till now, the darling child of Honour. (Dunlap 1799, p. 12)

ANDRE enters several minutes later (p. 18) to reinforce MELVILLE'S evaluations of him:

> KIND Heav'n be thank'd for that: I stand alone
>
> In this sad hour of life's brief pilgrimage!
>
> Single in misery; no one else involving
>
> In grief, in shame, and ruin. "'Tis my comfort .

Another character, unhappily named BLAND, and more unhappily one of the major characters, assures ANDRE that "thou shalt not die!" (p. 20), which leads into André's apologia:

> So did ambition lead me, step by step,
>
> To treat with traitors, and encourage treason;
>
> And then, bewilder'd in the guilty scene
>
> To quit my martial designating badges,
>
> Deny my name, and sink into the spy.
>
> (p. 22)

The unfortunate André is not only brave and noble, he is here self-contemptuous for dealing with traitors; the real André had been delighted at the prospect of enrolling such a high-ranking enemy, and couldn't wait to get possession of the plans of the fortifications at West Point. So anxious was he that he went in person, which act finally cost him his life. But on the New York stage BLAND reassures him, "Thou dids't no more than a soldier's duty" (p. 22). And so he had.

ANDRE knows that he must die—as in the actual life of the major we are primarily interested in his death, so on the stage ANDRE'S death is all—and it is his behavior in the shadow of this fact that creates his character. In the meantime, the audience must have its conventions. BLAND'S first effort is to reason with the GENERAL for ANDRÉ'S life, but that firm man refuses: "the destiny of millions, millions/Yet unborn, depends upon the rigor/Of this moment" (p. 31). But life is not going to be made any easier for GENERAL; MRS. BLAND and her two young children also seek an audience and beg him to spare ANDRE'S life: the life of her husband, in British hands, has been threatened in retaliation (she is BLAND'S mother). A BRITISH OFFICER arrives with threatening letters from Sir Henry Clinton.

ANDRE has meanwhile written to Sir Henry urging him against any retaliatory measures. A new character, McDONALD, not Washington's surrogate but certainly a representative of his argument, is nevertheless not swayed by the passion of BLAND and his mother. However, all will end nobly and happily (except for ANDRE, of course). Dunlap brings HONORA to America and has her visit the unfortunate ANDRE in prison; more bathos. But more is to come: BLAND'S father is released from prison—the British are more generous than we realized and than Dunlap admits—even though ANDRE'S hanging must proceed. His last words, on Dunlap's stage, show him a grown political scientist:

> But I must think your country has mistook
>
> Her interests. Believe me, but for this I should
>
> Not unwillingly have drawn a sword against her.
>
> (p. 60)

The final sentiments are those of BLAND, an American Dunlapian Kent:

> Farewell, farewell brave spirit. O, let my countrymen
>
> Henceforward, when the cruelties of war
>
> Arise in their remembrance; when their ready
>
> Speech would pour forth torrents in their foe's dispraise,
>
> Think on this act accurst, and lock complaint in silence.

André was produced at the Park Theater on March 30, 1778. It ran, as has already been noted, for only one night (although revived twice more, also for one night each). The play's misfortunes had to do with factors that were beyond the control of Dunlap and of André. The playwright did suggest in his preface that perhaps it was an unfortunate subject for the stage, it still being too near in time to the actual event; more time would have to elapse before André could be seen as a tragic figure. But nothing he wrote or did overcame that self-confessed handicap (so why did he write it?). The actors were dissatisfied with their parts. ANDRE was played Mr. Hodgkinson, BLAND by Thomas Cooper (no relation). At one point Cooper, who had forgotten his lines, called out "Oh, André, Oh André" and "falling in a burst of sorrow on Hodgkinson's neck, cried, loudly, `Oh, André—damn the prompter—Oh, André! What's next, Hodgkinson?'" (Odell, 1927, II:18).

André drew $817 that first night, a fair amount, but did not survive in its original form. It certainly could not save the Park from bankruptcy. It was revived a few years later as a musical, with some comedy added. Also added were the characters of the three irregulars who captured the unfortunate André, but their roles were comic (it was not billed as "André and the three stooges"); now called *The Glory of Columbia—Her Yeomanry,* its receipts for the first night were $1,287, but only $404 the next. *Glory* was repeated several times after 1803, but never stuck. After the outbreak of war in 1812, Dunlap added as a subtitle, "What We Have Done, We Can Do" (Odell 1927, II:181-82, 189, 390, 565).

Twenty-one years after his death, nearly a decade after the War of 1812, political relations were such that the British asked permission to disinter André's remains, for reburial in London. The American government, wanting to feel itself victorious in that recent war, magnanimously granted permission. In August 1821 a British detachment from the frigate *Phaeton,* which had sailed to America for that purpose, led by His Majesty's consul in New York, James Buchanan, removed André's bones from his unadorned grave in Tappan. His final place of entombment was to be Westminster Abbey.

Part Two

JAMES FENIMORE COOPER

8

The André Affair and *The Spy*

If Major André had not been captured in rebel-patrolled territory, out of uniform, and subsequently hanged, Cooper would never have written *The Spy;* or if he had, it would have been substantially different from the book he did write. The unhappy fate of that English officer had become a matter of great personal interest to the novelist; so great was his preoccupation with the André affair that Pickering (1971 Introduction to *The Spy*, pp. 22-23) called it a "hobby." The environs of Cooper's Westchester home were redolent with the history of André's complicity in Arnold's treason. Nearby was the modest house of Isaac Van Wart, one of André's captors, certainly a familiar object in Cooper's physical landscape. And if the Van Wart house did escape his attention, friend John Hatfield, an old-timer in the area, would most certainly have pointed it out to him. It was already an historic landmark.

André had become so much of a hobby for the novelist that he included a description of his mission, capture, and execution in his collection of essays, *Notions of the Americans*. They were near contemporaries, but not quite: Cooper had been born in 1789, nearly a decade after André's execution. *Notions* was his first book of nonfiction, written at the urging of Lafayette. The relevant essay is not merely an account of André's life as martyr but includes a lengthy defense of the Americans' actions. In a few pages Cooper summarizes André's mission and his capture. The arresting soldiers, characterized as Skinners—highwaymen—by some, are called "three young farmers" in *Notions*. The major lost his freedom because he failed to retain "his presence of mind," while the young Americans kept theirs (1828 I:280).

According to Cooper, when he "eagerly demanded" to know to which party they belonged, they "adroitly" answered, "below," to which André immediately confessed himself a British officer. This is not quite the way, more than two centuries after, we think it happened. Cooper, much closer to the actual event emotionally as well as chronologically, editorializes that had André "a quickness of intellect equal to the questionable office he had assumed, his miserable fate might have been averted" (1828 I:281).

Cooper says of the unfortunate André that his fate "became an object of the keenest solicitude to both armies" (1828 I:290). He supports the Americans in this matter; their leaders had from the beginning acted with "moderation and dignity" which gave their cause a character far nobler than that of a rebellion (1828 I:290). The struggle existed because men were fighting for the rights inherent in human nature, inalienable rights. That having been established, Cooper then defends the decision of the Americans to hang André. Treason is so repugnant "that he who is content to connect himself, ever so remotely, with its baseness, cannot expect to escape altogether from its odium" (1828 I:291). André's motives, Cooper found, were for his own personal preferment, and "he overstepped the coy and reserved distance which conscious dignity preserves ... and entered familiarly and personally into the details of the disgusting bargain" (1828 I:292). Cooper concluded that "it must be allowed that the case of Major André was one that can plead no such extraordinary exemption from the common and creditable feeling of mankind" (1828 I:293).

The decision to hang Major André was not fostered by vengeance, Cooper insisted, but involved loftier considerations of sovereignty:

> It was necessary to show the world that he who dared to assail the rights of the infant and struggling republics, incurred a penalty as fearful as he who worked his treason against the majesty of a king. The calmness, the humanity, the moderation, and the inflexible firmness, with which this serious duty was performed, are worthy of all praise. (1828 I:293-94)

While mounting his case of moral indignation against André and for his executioners, he did view the case with some balance. Cooper speaks of the "universal compassion" which was excited by the captive, which probably received some of its intensity in response to moral outrage over Arnold's treachery and escape. It required "no particular moral vision to see that the real criminal was free" (1828 I:294). And then Cooper makes the curious remark that Washington waited for some time in hopes of capturing Arnold and, by hanging him, appeasing justice. But when that did not happen, Cooper states, "it became necessary to let the law take its course" (1828 I:294). A stern morality pervades *Notions* (Cooper was, after all, a member of the Westchester County Bible Society and a vestryman of the church). James Beard writes (1960, p. xxiii) that *Notions* gives "an exaggerated, decidedly utopian impression of the moral and intellectual character of the American people," ignoring entirely those forces of social, economic, and political malaise which were waxing in the new republic. But that is not directly relevant to Major André.

The novelist's ambiguous feelings about "the unfortunate André" are revealed in *The Spy*. We have seen how, in *Notions of the Americans*, he detested the sin but admired the man. In the novel, the senior Wharton is appalled by the state of the world "when a man like Major André [can] lend themselves to the purposes of fraud." "Fraud!" his son replies excitedly, "surely, sir, you forget that Major André was serving his king, and that the usages of war [that phrase again!] justify the measure" (I:51). Cooper gives Captain Henry Wharton the argument the British defenders of André actually used. Before Henry's spy trial, Cooper brings up the analogy (and the contrast) with André again:

> The rank of André, and the importance of the measures he was plotting, together with the powerful intercessions that had been made on his behalf, occasioned his execution to be stamped with greater notoriety than the ordinary events of the war. But spies were frequently arrested, and the instances that occurred of summary punishment for this crime, were numberless. (II:143)

Cooper, through the voice of Frances, will not let the matter drop: "and did not the usages of war justify his death, Henry?" "Never!" he exclaimed (I:51). "On the subject of the death of André we are all of us uncommonly sensitive—you did not know him—he was all that was brave—that was accomplished—that was estimable" (I:52). And so that fictional family argument went, tossing and turning the defense and the vilification of André and his "affair."

Cooper concludes his evaluation of the affair with praise for the hanged man. There was but "one opinion" of his behavior: "it was highly noble and manly." André eschewed subterfuge or concealment; when the argument which would have bolstered his defense was suggested to him—that he had entered the American lines under the protection of a flag—he denied it, pointing out that if that had been so, he would have left under the same sanction. The court decided unanimously that he was guilty of spying, and he was sentenced to meet the fate of a spy: "he met his death heroically, and died amid the tears of all present" (1828 I:297).

Cooper accepted the judgment of the Board of Inquiry, and that of nearly all writers on the subject since: that André was guilty of being a spy, and according to the rules of war deserved to be hanged as one. In 1780 the Geneva Convention was more than a century away, the Hague Convention only a few years nearer (1899). Grotius wrote (1682) that unwritten laws "Such as Nature her self dictates ... are in force even in the midst of Arms" (p. xi). But according to those agreed-upon "rules of war," "a person can be considered to be a spy only when clandestinely or under false pretenses, he obtains or seeks to obtain information in the zone of operations of a belligerent for the purpose of communicating it to the other side." There must be, as Colonel C. Dewitt Willcox described the situation, a dissimulation, a violation of good faith (*Journal* 1904, p. 124). According to the Hague Accord—which formalized the rules of the conduct of war—a soldier in uniform may be a spy, and a combatant out of his military dress is not necessarily one. To justify execution, a spy must be captured within the enemy's lines; André was captured outside of the lines of both armies—he was in the No-Man's-

Land between the forces—and so in any event that his crime was capital was debatable.

The Board of Inquiry appointed by Washington seems to have been ignorant of these fine points—or they didn't care about them, because in the circumstances in which André was captured, they were interested primarily in hanging him. And the major himself seems to have been ignorant of a strict interpretation of the "rules" governing a definition of "spy." He never pointed out to his captors that his actions were not a violation of good faith, or that he had been captured between the lines. He had earlier been behind the American lines, to be sure; and this fact seems to have weighed on his conscience. He does not seem to have argued the difference between once having been within the enemy's lines and subsequently having been captured outside of them. And if the American officers who tried him were aware of his technical innocence, they certainly gave no indication of it. Major André was not a spy in purpose or intention; but Arnold's intended treason had frightened and infuriated the Americans, and they were not going to allow André to escape punishment. His hanging would discourage both the British (from ever trying such an adventure again) and other Americans (who might be considering such actions as Arnold succumbed to).

Cooper has no moral reflections about the Revolution's other famous spy, the young American, Nathan Hale. His execution did not take place so very close to Cooper's home as did André's, but that was not the principal cause of the novelist's lack of interest. Most of the nation felt that, compared to André, Hale was a spear carrier. Hale was a junior officer, a schoolteacher in civilian life; Major André was adjutant general of the British army. Hale had no prominent or important friends supporting him; and in any event, he was executed before news of his capture reached American lines. André's death excited great emotion on the part of both antagonists; Hale's did not. Yet it was a British journal, the *London Courant and Westminster Chronicle* (4 December 1780), that argued that the British army had set a dangerous precedent when it executed Nathan Hale in an "unceremonious manner," and had not even given him a decent burial (Seymour 1941, p. 300). Rank, then as now, had its privileges.

Hale volunteered for his last assignment following the battle of Long Island in the summer of 1776. Washington's beaten and dispirited army had retreated to New York, precariously holding the English at bay across the East River. The Continentals needed to know when the enemy intended to attack across that river, and precisely where. To this end Washington commanded Generals Heath and Clinton to set up an espionage network which would report continuously on British intentions: "As everything in a manner depends on obtaining intelligence of the enemy's motions," he wrote to Heath on 5 September, "I do most earnestly entreat you and General Clinton to exert yourselves to accomplish this most desirable end. Leave no stone unturned, nor do not stick at expense to bring this to pass" (Johnson, p. 93). Meanwhile, he was sending out small reconnaissance patrols with the dual function of gathering intelligence and of keeping the British off balance. These maneuvers were not effective. One particular unit, given such an assignment, was called "Knowlton's Rangers" after its commander; the unit and its missions interested the youthful patriot Nathan Hale.

He felt that his contribution to the Revolution had been slight, and desiring important action which would allow him to play a more important role, he offered his services when Colonel Knowlton asked for volunteers for an important spying mission. Hale was the only volunteer. He was aware of the consequences of discovery and capture, he told a friend: "But for a year I have ... not rendered any material service while receiving a compensation for which I make no return" (Johnston, pp. 100-101). He was not going to spy in the hope of a reward or promotion, but merely to "be useful, and every kind of service necessary to the public good, becomes honorable by being necessary" (ibid).

His penetration of British lines involved a roundabout route. From Westchester County he passed into his native Connecticut. (He had been born in Coventry, Connecticut, in June of 1755, and was graduated from Yale.) From Norwalk a boat ferried him across Long Island Sound. Landing on the island's north shore, he worked his way to Hempstead, where he took off his uniform and donned an innocent brown suit and broad-brimmed hat. His cover, which matched his new garb, was that of a Dutch schoolmaster. In civilian life he had been a teacher. When behind enemy lines, he learned that the Continentals had recently been defeated in battle and had been forced to retire to the north of Haarlem heights. The intelligence that he had been sent to report was now irrelevant; nevertheless he continued with his now altered mission, assuming that any information he could gather about British troop movements would be useful.

Hale, still in disguise, moved to the area just south of Haarlem where the British were digging in following their recent victory over the Continentals. Here he was captured, though details are murky and contradictory; the British never thought his case interesting or important enough to begin an investigation of his movements. Apparently he tried to pass through British lines, was taken by their pickets, and almost immediately identified as a spy. Not only did he have in his possession sketches of fortifications (which he had himself drawn), but he confessed. One tradition has it that Hale was recognized by a Tory cousin, who chanced to be in New York on business, Samuel Hale, and denounced to the British. A variant of this legend has it that cousin Samuel identified him after his capture (Seymour, pp. 304-305). This detail seems to have been invented to create in this tragedy a Judas figure whose role in the Hale martyrdom is solely to act as the betrayer of the innocent patriot. No matter; in the event, the British had the evidence of the incriminating papers, and that was enough to hang him. And hang him they did, on 22 September, 1776. Ironically, just a month before Hale's mission, friend Betsy Hallam had sent him a letter in which she quoted Addison's *Cato* to the effect that death in defense of one's country was "glorious" (Seymour, p. 85).

Like André, Hale's deportment just prior to his execution aroused the sympathy of those who got to know him. We owe to British officer John Montresor the rendering of Hale's (supposed) last words, later allegedly repeated to American Captain William Hull. The *London Courant and Westminster Chronicle* has it differently: Montresor, a general, under a flag of truce recited an account of Hale's last hours to Washington personally. However these famous last words were allegedly transmitted, they sound apocryphal, the kind of utterance designed to arouse American patriotic spirit. In them Nathan Hale becomes an exemplar of selfless devotion to duty, as André was of superior poise and courage while in the hands of barbarians; the unfortunate major symbolizes the defeat of a superior culture by its intellectual and moral inferiors.

The era abounds with symbols. Cooper makes Harvey Birch's soul noble, the peddler an exemplar of patriotism and democratic zeal. The War of Independence, many felt (including André), was really a "civil war," replicated in the War of 1812. "Revolution" is a recurring theme—later in the "Frontier," the "New Frontier," the "Last Frontier," and so on.

Hale's unsuitability to espionage should be attributed to his modesty, his piety, his inherent naiveté. After such a heroic death his character would naturally be greatly extolled and extravagantly embellished—as was André's—yet his guilelessness did strike many of those who knew him as paramount. Elizabeth Poole of New London thought him

> particularly free from the shadow of guile! His remarkably expressive features were an index of the mind & heart that every new emotion lighted with a brilliancy perceptible to even common observers. No species of deception had any lurking-place in his frank, open, meek & pious mind; his soul disdained disguise, however imperious circumstances of personal safety might demand a resort to duplicity & ambiguity. (Seymour 1941, p. 160)

Honest Hale was conspicuously naive, and therefore ill-suited to the treacherous business of espionage; his character was insurance against effective spying. One poet posthumously lauded him as "removed from envy, malice, pride and strife,/He walked through goodness as he walked through life;/A kinder brother nature never knew,/A child more duteous, or a friend more true" (in Seymour, p. 358). André, an officer and gentleman, did not deserve hanging because his was a gallant and noble character.

The Spy did not come easily to Cooper. Grossman (1949, p. 17) repeats the legend that one evening while reading aloud to his wife, Susan, he disgustedly threw the book aside with the remark that he could write better than that himself. This must have seemed more of an unlikely claim than it appears on the surface of it, since he did not like to write at all; he even disliked writing letters. This attitude changed dramatically; after a writing career of three decades he had finished thirty-two novels and a dozen other books. His first literary effort was a short moral tale that so dissatisfied him that he tore it up. *Precaution,* usually thought of as his first book, was actually the second, though it is the first to survive and to be published.

The matter of his literary ambitions is slightly more complex than that; Cooper wrote to Andrew Thompson Goodrich, an acquaintance and his publisher, that his tale had swelled to "a rather unwieldly size" (Beard 1960, I:42), and that he destroyed the manuscript and "chang'd it to a novel." With that narrative still in his mind, he began work on *The Spy* during 1820. However, before much work had been done on it he set it aside as being too venturesome. The first volume had actually been printed when he decided to let the project rest. He first thought to abandon the book entirely, but was persuaded to continue because of complimentary reviews received in England for *Precaution.* Its reception would be a guarantee against loss (Grossman 1949, p. 23). He wanted very much for *The Spy* (as well as for his subsequent books) to be successes. Having let the narrative settle in his mind for several months, he resumed work on it in early 1821. In a letter of 28 June 1820 to Andrew Thompson Goodrich, Cooper speaks of the sixty pages of the book that have been finished (Beard 1960, I:44). Written very quickly, they were set aside without much anguish.

He complained that "the task of making American Manners and American scenes interesting to an American reader is an arduous one—I am unable to say whether I shall succeed or not" (Beard 1960, pp. 44-45). And a few weeks later—6 July—he wrote to Goodrich seeking his opinion of "The Spy," "a work which will be vastly more popular than 'Precaution' or intolerable and which of the two I really don't know" (Beard 1960, p. 46). In the same letter he lamented that the book was certainly "written hastily," but that the style "is not bad." He cites a friend, James Aitchison (to whom *The Spy* was dedicated) as having pronounced it "well adapted to the kind of book," which had been the author's aim all along.

Dissatisfaction with the first book soon set in; and with it optimism for that which was forthcoming. Some proof sheets of the new novel would enable him to correct his pages more thoroughly; he was at the moment (July 1820) busy with the harvest, but he vowed that he "can attend" to it in the evenings. He thought *Precaution* so "very—very—inferior" to "The Spy" that he had given up hopes of its success. Grossman thinks that *Precaution* was "very bad" (1949, p. 19). Nevertheless, since it was a moral book, which, he granted, "The Spy" was not, he expected that it would have good sales. Morality in fiction was an important matter with him; fictional writings were "formidable weapons in the cause of morality" (Beard 1960, p. xxii). And he assumed that morality would be as important with his readers. Goodrich's questions about some stylistic matters ("peculiarities of style") induced Cooper to request his professional advice. He was genuinely baffled since he had aimed at "simplicity and clearness," though, since it had been written hastily, the book might have some problems. Cooper thought it possible that some grammatical errors might have crept into the text, so hastily had "The Spy" been written (Beard 1960, p. 48).

After its early compositional swiftness, "The Spy" went slowly for him (as he complained to Goodrich on 12 July); he had had models for *Precaution*—Jane Austen's *Persuasion* and to some extent *Pride and Prejudice*. He had none for "The Spy" and he did not expect to finish it until late in the fall. But, he wanted to assure his publisher, he thought that it a "far better" novel than *Precaution*: it was more interesting, he thought, and had in it "better writing." Later (19-20 October) he admitted to Goodrich that the novel's plot had not been decided on until after the first volume had been half done (Beard 1960, p. 66). He wrote the last chapter—a kind of epigraph to the novel and almost an irrelevance to the plot—before the last several chapters that immediately preceded it had been thought of; this to reassure Goodrich.

9

André and Cooper

Daughter Susan Cooper remembered that her father was fond of chatting with the older residents of the area, gathering what we would now call oral data about Revolutionary days. And he would invite neighbors over to his house, Angevine, and note carefully what they said about life in the old Revolutionary times. He also interviewed several people who worked for him around the estate. He included an account of André's apprehension and death in his *Notions of the Americans*. And several years after the publication of *The Spy*, in 1834, when showing an English guest, Charles A. Murray, the region of the upper Hudson, he knowledgeably pointed out various parts of the topography relevant to André's last days.

South of Cooper's home is the village of Tappan, where André was tried, imprisoned while awaiting sentencing, hanged, and initially buried. The town is still a small one, though most of its growth has been in the profusion of private houses which now surround the historic village. Washington is clearly its hero of choice, and much of Tappan's historical consciousness concerns the general's having once headquartered there. There is a Washington Street, a Washington Lane, and a Washington Avenue. The DeClark-DeWint house, the oldest in Rockland County, said to have been used by Washington on four different occasions, is well preserved on a well-manicured several acre plot. It is handsomely landscaped and inside provisioned with furniture of the era.

But André's memory in Tappan (the Historical Society refers to the village in its Revolutionary days as "Tappantown") has not been overlooked. Washington is appropriately the town's hero, but Major André's execution has been the biggest event in the area's history. The Mabie house, where André was held captive, still stands. Built by Casparus Mabie in 1755, and first used as a tavern in 1800 by Philip DuBuy, it has again become a tavern and restaurant. The present owner has remodeled the interior and removed the walls which once comprised the chamber in which André was held. A large wooden frame dining area has been built in back, though the front of the structure—now called the "1776 House"—is of the same brownstone that it was during the Revolution.

The building in which the Court of Inquiry held its investigation and deliberations is the reformed church building. The first church was built on this site in 1694; the second church was the venue of the André trial. The present structure is the fourth church, still standing adjacent to the old town burying grounds, across from the village green in the village center.

From the Mabie house where he was incarcerated, André was marched to his death, about a mile, up a slight incline, to a waiting gallows. The tree which is said by natives to have been used for the occasion no longer exists. The site is a small cleared area with a roadway around it, serving as a horseshoe lane for several suburban (exurban would be more accurate) homes. The event is marked by a squared, beveled concrete monument, about three feet high. A wrought-iron fence—about fifteen feet in diameter—surrounds the monument, and contains patches of ignored grass and weeds. Locals think that André was first buried here as well. The road to this monument is marked by a New York State historical sign pointing toward where several comfortable, recently built suburban houses are sited, and to the place where the spy was hanged.

James Fenimore Cooper's second novel, *The Spy*, praised by contemporaries because it dealt with American subjects, mentions André several times, though he is not a character in the novel. Significantly, three of Cooper's characters appear in disguise, often behind enemy lines; a fourth does not disguise his appearance, but lies about his marital status in order to court one of the novel's heroines. The book seems to be an argument about the nature and the character of clandestinity; when is it innocuous and when culpable? George Washington appears several times in the guise of "Mister Harper." No blame is attached to him; and the spy of the title, Harvey Birch, is one of Cooper's noblest and actively patriotic characters. Another "spy," Henry Wharton, travels behind the American lines out of uniform in order to visit his father and sisters whose house is in the "Neutral Ground."

Wharton's situation parallels that of André in several respects: he too has come into the upper Hudson valley from the British strong point in New York City; both men arrived at their destinations on board British warships, both were left stranded when their ships were forced to sail downstream, and both men attempt to escape back to their lines out of uniform—in disguise. Both are captured; and Wharton is tried as a common spy (as was André), in an emotional scene that is explicitly redolent of the real British officer's plight.

Through the development of these characters and their fictional situations, Cooper investigates the morality (and variety of intention) of disguises in wartime. Wharton's motives are innocent, and his civilian disguise is perpetrated for an act of nobility—to succor his aging father and his two nearly helpless sisters. Major André's purposes were criminal and contrary to the laws of the new republic; thus André was appropriately hanged (Cooper seems to imply) while Wharton is allowed to escape from his prison (with the aid of Harvey Birch—the "spy" of the title) and to be escorted back to the safety of the British lines.

British Colonel Wellmere is disreputable in several respects. He is a braggart and a malingerer; and while he does not adopt a disguise (or alter his physical appearance), he does dissemble about his private life. His deceives with wicked intent. He leads the Whartons to believe that he is a bachelor so that he may court one of the Wharton daughters. Only a surprise announcement by Harvey Birch exposes him, and shame drives him from the Wharton home.

The spy of the title is not André, however, or anything like him, although the British major does hover, invisibly and prominently, in the background of the text. Harvey Birch was poor and ignorant, so far as formal education went, but a shrewd man and self-possessed and fearless—ideal for a spy. His continuing assignment was to observe "in what part of the country the agents of the crown were making their effort to embody men, to repair to the place, enlist, appear zealous in the cause he affected to serve," and in general to learn as many secrets of and about the British as he could (from the 1849 Preface cited in Pickering 1971, p. 14). And in concluding remarks that would hardly be necessary today, Cooper summarized the final phase of Birch's mission as informing "his employers" of his intelligence so that they might act to counter British intentions. They were often successful.

Cooper's acquaintance, John Jay—he was a friend of Cooper's father, Judge William Cooper—"ran" his agent during the Revolution until he was himself reassigned overseas, on a diplomatic mission to Spain. But he never, even many years after the war, revealed his name—as well he shouldn't. "All throughout his years of service, the man stubbornly refused money; his patriotism wasn't to be bought" (Pickering 1971, p. 14). This is especially impressive in light of the usual practice of spies and rewards for them, summarized by Napoleon's famous dictum that the only proper reward for a spy was gold.

From Elizabeth De Lancey (Cooper had married a De Lancey—Susan Augusta) he would have gotten much of the Revolutionary lore about spies which he used in formulating the background, character, and life style of Harvey Birch. Elizabeth Floyd, later to be the novelist's mother-in-law, was a frequent guest at the De Lanceys'. Mary Floyd was married (since 1784) to Colonel Benjamin Tallmadge, an upper-level director of Washington's secret service. After André's execution in the fall of 1780, Oliver De Lancey, Jr., was promoted to his post; Oliver had been, in effect, André's executive officer for intelligence matters, the officer in specific charge of intelligence, as Flexner describes him (1953, p. 328). So, just within his own extended family, Cooper had access to a great deal of material about spying during the Revolution. We should therefore not be at all surprised when Pickering says that "the immediate sources of the novel, it seems fairly certain, were primarily of an oral nature" (1971, p. 20). Yet knowing the immediate sources, obviously, does not enable us to get a firm grip on the novel.

Tallmadge ran a network in what is now the metropolitan New York area, including Long Island and Westchester. His two most effective agents, Robert Townsend and Abraham Woodhull, were known for decades after by their code names, Culper Junior and Culper Senior, respectively. Townsend was Tallmadge's agent in place; posing as a New York City merchant, he gathered data and transmitted what he considered to be relevant to Woodhull via courier. The latter, Culper Senior, was the final transmission link, arranging for the intelligence to be taken by small boat across Long Island Sound to Tallmadge in Westchester.

The concept of espionage was much simpler in that relatively innocent time, and the world was more easily understood. Today "spying" can mean the gathering of information, catching the enemy's spies, or covert action. This last category actually includes a wide range of activities: assassinations, bribery, the conduct of black propaganda, the overthrow of governments, and counterinsurgency activities. Spies clandestinely tap our telephone lines, haul disabled aircraft out of the ocean, bribe pilots from the "other side" to fly their aircraft (or drive their tanks) to our bases; spies give decoding machines to alien nations (the spies of other nations had devised them in the first place), they plan methods for making Castro's beard fall out, thus supposedly discrediting him to his people.

In Cooper's day a spy could be either something like a scout or a lookout—one who observed others, or who observed terrain so as to be prepared for hostile activity, or one who observed foreign (or distant) land and military fortifications, or the activity of a potential enemy.

The latter duty does not seem very different from the activities of some agents today, but for the most part a spy's activities in the early nineteenth century were less insidious. James Pattie reports that at one bivouac in territory in which the men feared an Indian attack, they made breastworks and "posted spies in the limbs of the tall trees" who would warn of approaching Indians (1984 rpt. p. 86). These spies are lookouts, or guards: overt, they do not operate clandestinely in a potential or real enemy's territory.

Pattie subsequently met with an Indian chief sometime in the late 1820s who told him about his tribe's relations with the Spanish. After great numbers of them had been slaughtered by the invaders, the Indians sent several of their number to live among the Spaniards, even consenting to be baptized so as not to arouse suspicion. But these "agents in place," as we would now call them, "remain faithful spies for us, informing us when and where there were favorable opportunities to kill, and plunder our enemies" (1984 rpt. p. 70).

Later, when entering Spanish California, the locals were suspicious, and Pattie and his companions were obliged to show their passports, "proving" that they were "neither robbers, murderers, nor spies" (pp. 151-52). Pattie and his company were not spies, but their innocence was not believed, and they were imprisoned nevertheless: they were considered "worse then thieves and murderers." They were thought to be "spies for the old Spaniards, and that [their] business was to lurk about the country, that [they] might inspect the weak and defenseless points of the frontiers, and point them out to the Spanish, in order that they might introduce their troops into the country" (p. 158).

During an expedition through the Southwest, an Apache confided to Josiah Gregg (1967 rpt. p. 116) that they knew that his tribesmen could not defeat the Spaniards in open battle. Experience had taught them that much. So they decided to overcome the enemy—actually a potential enemy since the war between their groups was a "cold war"—by subterfuge. "By conversing with the enemy the spies had been able to ascertain their temper and their projects" (1967 rpt. p. 116). The attackers were confident of success: the god of the Christians, they assured him, was dead; their god was immortal.

At an earlier moment, Gregg (pp. 5-6) noted that after the capture and execution of Hidalgo all foreigners, but especially Americans, were viewed with suspicion by the Spanish government. One of the results was that some of the first traders with Santa Fé were seized as spies, all of their goods confiscated, and themselves imprisoned (anticipating the fate of Pattie and his party some two decades later).

This kind of clandestine activity, if true, would be a serious threat to the resident government—that kind of insidious spying which threatens a foreign power, and not at all the kind of spying/observing that was as common in Cooper's day. That activity was relatively innocuous. Nobody would be hanged for observing the landscape, scanning for potential enemies. This is the kind of activity that the titular wooden-legged spy in L. A. Jones' 1909 dime novel engaged in; the German spy scare in England which led to the creation of the British Secret Service had not yet infected the United States, where spying was for the most part a protective, overt action.

Cooper is the acknowledged originator of the popular, literary, Western novel. Henry Nash Smith and John Cawelti have discussed this development in some detail. Smith *(Virgin Land* 1970, pp. 59ff.) establishes Cooper's Leatherstocking as the archetypal Western hero, even though he is never made to travel west of the Mississippi. Based loosely on the popular life of Daniel Boone, Cooper's Leatherstocking became, in Smith's opinion, "by far the most important symbol of the national experience of adventure across the continent" (p. 61). An inveterate woodsman, Leatherstocking epitomized the life of independence, a freedom from the constraint of law, and its lack of ceremony.

From the first, Cooper's conception of his hero was ambiguous. Because Leatherstocking lived in the forest, his life symbolized liberty and freedom from societal restraint. Yet Cooper had to make him a worthy character; he made him one of nature's gentlemen, yet also made him speak in a dialect that would mark him immediately as unschooled. Inherently good, the woodsman was not socially acceptable enough to get to marry the heroine. She was always, in Cooper's novels, delicately genteel. Cooper could not create a hero who could surmount this social barrier and thus be worthy to wed the lady, despite his innate quality of character. And this failure, Smith thought, was ultimately Cooper's weakness. A more inventive novelist might have devised a new fictional form, but "Cooper was not the man to undertake a revolution, either in life or in literature" (p. 64).

The novelist had similar problems with *The Spy,* though that novel had been an enormous success. Harvey Birch was not an appropriate hero; his occupation (peddler as well as spy) negated that option. And yet he is heroic and fiercely patriotic. As Smith says, for Cooper's age a novel was a love story (p. 65). Birch does not have—could not have—a romantic interest. That success is reserved for Major Dunwoodie. The Wharton daughters are suitable matches only for gentlemen, leaving Harvey only his work—which is always by its nature suspect. As Cooper could not overcome the contradictions inherent in his formula of the independent woodsman who was socially inferior to his better-educated, socially prominent peers, earlier he certainly could not deal with Harvey Birch as hero. Society could not accept such an idea; and Cooper could not give such a figure a life other than one of isolation and sordid secrecy.

Charles Averill's *Kit Carson, The Prince of the Gold Hunters* is seen (by Smith, p. 88) as a transposition of Cooper's hero to the West, where he is similarly garbed and situated and called "Kit Carson." The novel's situation is straight out of Cooper: the genteel hero, an appropriately nurtured heroine, villains, and the "faithful guide." Averill had learned one fictive lesson; he subordinated his Eastern hero while elevating the character of Kit. And he made his hero a Westerner, not the woodsman of Cooper's Eastern forests. Carson is a young man, mounted, daily coping with a world and a landscape that are not benign, but continually posing danger. This is the hero and his milieu (Smith thought, p. 89) which was to influence the image and the setting of the Western story for the next half-century.

Orville Victor, publishers Beadle and Adams' most successful editor, is said to have told a reporter that the Beadle stories "followed right after Cooper's tales" (Smith, p. 92). Specifically this meant that the character of the mature huntsman proliferated. In the tradition of Averill's Cooper adaptation, these Leatherstocking descendants carried a flintlock rifle, wore moccasins, rode horseback, and never hesitated to rescue genteel ladies from Indian captivity. Even the character of Buffalo Bill did not achieve independence, but in the pages of Ned Buntline's fictions became yet another of Leatherstocking's kin. Bill's English is quite correct—at times elegant—and dialect is reserved for other characters. Yet Bill's adventures include the rescue of genteel maidens from the

Indians, which his expert woodsmanship (or is it plainsmanship?) accomplishes by outcrafting the Indians. Cooper was alive and well in the Far West.

Cawelti's highly successful and satisfying attempt to define a literary genre—some would say "subliterary"—in *The Six-Gun Mystique,* talks about the literary genre of the Western in terms of personae and setting. The Western has three individuals or groups of them, defined by their function within the narrative: (1) the townies, who represent civilization and who dwell within a village or town which is set in the Western prairies or mountains (2) the hero, usually one individual, although his function can be multiplied, who mediates between the townies; and (3) the representatives of destruction and/or chaos, usually Indians or outlaws.

The destroyers—the "savages," as Frederick Jackson Turner and a great many others have polarized them—are mobile and free-ranging. They have no permanent home, no fixed abode, just a nomadic lodging, no commitment to societal stability. The townies—unless they are overland trail voyagers, and as such are considered bringers of civilization—are confined to immovable dwellings; they have an investment in the land and in permanent living quarters. The hero(es)have the outlaws or the Indians' mobility, but they lend their services to the bringers of civilization, whether farmers or ranchers or settlement dwellers. In respect to their means of mobility and their attitudes toward permanent dwelling, they are mediaries. The hero may relieve the town of its imminent danger, but will ride off into the sunset.

Cawelti identifies Cooper as the first writer of Westerns because he was the first writer to bring all three character types together within the Western landscape (p. 41). The latter consideration especially shows how much Cawelti is influenced by the film's rendering of the Western. Nevertheless, Cooper's importance and his influence on the genesis and development of this literary genre is detailed.

In this definition of the Western, the forces of civilization "must" prevail (Cawelti, p. 36). "Savagery" must inevitably be overcome; and so the town is not seen as an isolated outpost in the wilds, but a settlement temporarily apart from the main forces of civilization. This is characteristic of the Western as film and of fictions created after the fact of the "winning" of the frontier. One would not think of a frontier settlement—with its false building facades and its wooden plank streets—as seriously threatened, because we know that in the historic life-world they did persevere. But the Western formula, originating in Cooper, did change during the latter half of the nineteenth century. At first, in Cooper, the wilderness (though of the East and not the trans-Mississippi West) was a staging point for a confrontation between man and nature, but after mid-century (when it was universally felt that "civilization" must inevitably win), the Western was modified: the formulas remained though the issue was no longer the prevalence of man or the survival of societal structure.

10

Cooper and the Spy Novel

Cooper also gave us the first spy novel, a genre whose time has finally come round at last. Many spy novelists today—Eric Ambler and John Le Carré, for instance, credit John Buchan as being their creative inspiration. Probably they too had never read an American book, certainly not Cooper's. So, many of Cooper's insights, and many of those quite remarkable, had to be relived, and the fictional garb in which he clothed them reinvented.

Cooper was the first writer to depict the spy's isolation. Harvey Birch, in *The Spy*, lives with an aging father and a cleaning woman who is ignorant of his beliefs and of his occupation in the "Neutral Ground." He does not seem to have friends; certainly he can only confide in "Harper" (General Washington) about his work. Only Washington knows the true nature of Birch's work, and he cannot reveal this to anyone. Birch's patriotism must proceed unrecognized and unappreciated by his countrymen, who were often the very people who distrusted and reviled him. Cooper is by no means neutral or dispassionate in his evaluation of some mask-wearers: some of his fellow-citizens, "stigmatized as a foe, have been useful agents"; while others, who have masqueraded as "flaming patriots," were all along under royal protection, and were actually "concealed under piles of British gold" (Cooper 1821, p. 2).

Closely related is the perception that the spy is an island cut loose from his surroundings, adrift in his world, however temporarily. In Cooper's Neutral Ground many people were in that situation, fearful of revealing their true feelings or affiliations. In an often-quoted passage—especially important for this book—Cooper describes the situation of "a large proportion" of the Neutral Ground dwellers as inhabitants "either restrained by their attachments or influenced by their fears," who pretended a neutrality that was not always felt; a great many "wore masks, which even to this day [1821] have not been thrown aside" (Cooper 1821, p. 2). Of course he is alluding to Harvey Birch, who dwelled in the Neutral Ground, and who will be introduced to the reader shortly. But he is also describing the tenor of life among the noncombatants in "West-Chester" county during 1780 and 1781. They too, those who were not spies, were not involved in the war in any direct way, did not give aid or comfort to either side (except, perhaps, in some cases, emotional), they were also terrorized into a kind of facade of neutrality.

In Cooper's novel, Washington-as-Harper seeks shelter from a swiftly rising storm at the first place he comes across; it is Birch's, though its owner is not at home. Harvey's housekeeper sends the needy stranger onto the Whartons', where—she assures him—he will be welcomed hospitably. When he arrives there and is soon settled in congenial conversation with the Wharton patriarch, they lament that the war has made the availability of tobacco difficult. Harper's part in this conversation has to be seen with a certain measure of irony. But the elder Wharton is given a line, which although about tobacco, reveals his understanding of his situation in the Neutral Ground: the war had made any sort of communication with New York City, however innocent, "too dangerous to be risked," especially for so trifling a matter as tobacco (Cooper 1821, p. 8).

The spy cannot function—in some instances he will not survive—without invisibility. Harvey Birch is so productive a spy because his pretended occupation—that of peddler— enables him to travel from post to post, from city to country, passing through each army's lines because of his ordinariness, and that degree of inconspicuousness allows him to move freely from place to place. Birch attracts little notice; both the British and the colonists suspect him, but for most of the novel he is allowed to travel at will. His mobility is that of many other itinerant peddlers. One of André's most successful spies, after all, Ann Bates, had also disguised herself as a peddler when she explored the colonists' positions to the north of New York City.

Cooper seems to have understood the spy's precarious existence in No-Man's-Land, and he understood it in a way and to a degree and in such detail that is astonishingly modern. The spy—Harvey Birch, like the spies of contemporary fiction—is a creature of the night. Not the least of Cooper's perceptions concern the "Neutral Ground," and the psychology of those who live there. His own home was in Westchester County, and many of his neighbors remembered what wartime in the region was like. Cooper did not invent "No-Man's-Land"—that was a product of the European imagination at least as old as the fourteenth century—and probably earlier—the region from which exiles were sent forth and where felons were hanged. But Cooper's treatment of life in such an area shows that he could recreate such a mental environment in his writing, and populate it with people whose lives were constantly on the verge of disruption, betrayal, anarchy, unforeseen violence, even chaos.

11

The McDonald Papers

This vision of chaos was not conceived entirely out of Cooper's imagination; his model was Westchester County, where he spent a good many of his adult years, itself a neutral ground during the Revolution. Thanks to a collection of reminiscences by residents collected and transcribed by a Dr. J. M. McDonald in 1844-47, we can reconstruct some idea of what the area must have been like in the 1780s. These oral histories are uneven in that McDonald does not seem to have had a particular organizing principle in collecting; and none of the informants is identified. It is as though this collection were made for other residents in Westchester, all of whom would know of the characters mentioned in the anecdotes by name; for them no identification would be necessary. If Dr. McDonald had in mind to write a complete oral history of Westchester during the Revolution, none has survived, and no mention of one has ever been found.

Many of the informants locate their stories at some time during 1780 or 1781; McDonald's collection is dated 1844 (and for several years following). The informants, therefore, would have been at least eighty-four years old at the time (assuming that they were twenty in 1780). Their memories would necessarily be faulty, the details blurred. And it is clear from McDonald's transcription that he has polished up their narrative styles; in a few cases he has prompted his informants, or edited their errors. Whether or not he added or altered significant details cannot be known. Nevertheless, despite all these possibilities for misrepresentation, exaggeration, and understatement, for error plain and simple, these reminiscences do provide, collectively, an idea of what life must have been like in Westchester County during 1780 and 1781.

The British army was based in New York City, and often enough sallied forth to do battle in the No-Man's-Land north of them. Two of McDonald's informants, John and Isaiah Coutant, remembered the opening shots:

> The British army first encamped from Elias Guion's farm to Haerlem river, and then on our farm along the Ridge. Howe's Headquarters were at James Angsleys, father of Hannah, an old house on the east side of the road to White Plains, a little north of the cross road leading to our house. The skirmish with the Hessians took place at the house where the widow Morrell kept a tavern, and the wounded were brought all the way to our house to have their wounds dressed. The firing created a great alarm, and the British regiments all turned out. (I:8-9)

Ezra Lockwood and Mrs. Hunt were more graphic and detailed in their account of armed combat. Their narrative ends with an anecdote (illustrating poise under fire, and quick-wittedness, among other qualities), but is polished enough that McDonald's editing may be suspected. At the least, the story shows that Lockwood/Hunt had had a great deal of time to perfect their narrative. Its punchline ending suggests that it was a well-remembered story probably told and retold many times in the six decades since its actual occurrence. It happened on a night so stormy that no one expected enemy action Major Tallmadge nevertheless rode out with a scouting party to reconnoiter the land.

> About half a mile from Poundridge, on rising a hill, he suddenly met the British advanced guard face to face. They had previously been hid from him by the winding of the road and the hills. He wheeled about with his command and retreated, the British following at full gallop, shouting and screeching: "Surrender! you damned Rebels, surrender! &. In this way they entered Poundridge. Sheldon's [party] [stationed nearby, in the path of the attacking British] seeing themselves outnumbered and being surprised wheeled and retreated South upon the Stamford road the British following and charging whenever they could .... There were many fights along the wood. There was a private in Sheldon's named Buckhout who was called upon repeatedly to surrender but refused.

The dragoon threatened to shoot but he still refused. At last the dragoon fired exclaiming: "There, you damned Rebel!—A little more and I would have shot you dead!" The bullet had just grazed his cheek. Buckhout instantly and promptly replied: "Yes, damn you! and a little more and you would not have hit me at all." (I:83-85)

Small units frequently made raids to the north; spies and other mysterious people commonly came ashore from whaleboats (and other vessels); residents could not tell who these people were, on whose side they fought, or what their missions were. These small but swift boats also served (occasionally) as men-of-war in the small wars at sea. Madam Mead, as she is identified by McDonald, told about her husband's duty at sea, when Congress "authorized and recommended retaliation by whaleboats" on the British vessels in the Sound, which was "infested with plunderers" (I:71). The Continentals too made raids to the south and seem to have been engaged in an active commerce with the whaleboat people. On occasion, small units acted on their own behind enemy lines, much as they did in Vietnam:

> One of *Delancey's men* was up with a flag and talking of some prisoners they had recently made, said to Cornelius Oakley: "We'll have you next."—Oakley replied, "That may well be, for none of us can tell what may happen." He soon after received information from a spy (a cripple who was suffered to go about among the Refugee posts and settlements unmolested and unsuspected) that there was to be a great ball at a house near fort No. 8. Oakley, and a party went down on the appointed night. They passed the advanced posts undiscovered, and crept along a wall by Redoubt No. 8, close to the sentinels and reached the house in question, without being seen or heard. The revelers were completely surprised, being engaged in dancing while they surrounded the house and up to the moment when they entered. The men were seized before they could get their arms and threatened with death if they resisted. The women shrieked, and a scene ensued when their partners were captured, but they brought off most, if not all, the prisoners. The garrison of No. 8 was alarmed, and pursued; but Oakley's party retreated successfully, having taken among other prisoners the very man who predicted his (Oakley's) capture. (I:18-19)

In the field, in actual combat, prisoners were often a burden. They were sometimes killed as soon as captured; if they were spared they often tried to escape, often successfully. John Carpenter told McDonald about one such evasion (which makes the escapes in Cooper's novel seem quite commonplace) after he and Colonel Thomas were caught and imprisoned in a private house; the story is related in the third person:

> Col. Thomas told Carpenter he would jump from the window, and Carpenter said he would follow. Thomas sprang like a squirrel upon (or in) a small pen, and instantly a cry arose: "One of them has escaped! Shoot! Kill him! One hundred shots were fired but he escaped westerly to a swamp covered with trees and brush, but closely followed by some horsemen, when, unfortunately, he came into the midst of Ogden's troop who were in pursuit of Reuben Lane, one of Thomas's party who had escaped. He, clung to the neck of Ogden's horse. Ogden held his sword over and protected him for which Thomas afterwards showed himself grateful. Thomas was in his shirt and drawers when he attempted to escape, in which dress they took him off. (I:43)

Thomas Carpenter was with Colonel Thomas when he and his brother made their escapes; but he chose not to follow those two out of the window, crawling under a convenient bed instead. When he was found there, he was persistently bayoneted, and when he finally surrendered, he was taken out to the road to die. But friends retrieved him and brought him to his house, where his wife was nursing him, when one of General Parsons' own surgeons, escorting the general who happened to ride by, came in and dressed his numerous wounds.

The British had inadvertently left one of their wounded near Thomas' house, and two troopers were sent back to fetch him. As they were carrying him along, an old woman taunted them: "You've got a fine parcel of plunder there!" (I:44).

Killing and burning were commonplace. Zacchaus Mead recalled one skirmish in which several British cavalry rode up to a colonial guardhouse and ordered the occupants to surrender; when they answered with a volley, the English officer in charge was seriously wounded (dying shortly after); his men set fire to the guardhouse, and then rode down the men who fled. Then they set fire to a nearby house "near a church belonging to two brothers named Smith":

> This house is said to have been burnt at the instigation of Lockwood, one of Delancey's (Fowler's) men who was from Horseneck and had had a quarrel with the Smiths. An infirm woman in the second story was burnt to death. Two barns were burnt at the same time which caught fire from the two houses. Five of the guard were killed and a number wounded—two mortally. Delancey took some of the troops prisoner and a number of the inhabitants were taken off. The refugees broke the windows of the houses of obnoxious persons when they retreated. (I:56-57)

Burning and killing were a common experience in the neutral ground. Civilians became instant combatants—as in Vietnam—and no one, regardless of appearances, could be trusted. Mrs. Patty Holmes of Bedford saw it this way:

> Poundridge was burnt on Friday, and Bedford ... nine days after. On the retiring of the British from Poundridge through Bedford they burnt the church, that is the Meeting House and Colonel Holmes' house, and a week from the next Sunday they burnt all the houses, except one. A woman begged them to spare her house and they consented. She then interceded for the opposite house where the brothers of Colonel Holmes lived. Here they found a pair of pistols, and would not then consent. &. The British were part refugees and part regular troops. When the British retreated from Poundridge Capt. Gilbert Dean's first wife attacked and took a Refugee soldier who lagged behind. Armed with her husband's gun she made him prisoner. (I:88)

Especially at night the irregulars—the privateers—of both sides, cowboys and skinners, roamed at will, looting, pillaging, killing. McDonald more politely referred to them as "foragers." They took from their friends, McDonald quotes Lott Merritt as saying (I:31), but when they did so "they gave certificates which were afterwards paid."

The Coutants further remembered that *"Shube Merritt* belonged to Emmerick, but conducted himself so bad that Emmerick dismissed him, and he then fought and plundered upon his own hook, as a cowboy. He lost one hand and part of his forearm, and was killed at [Mrs. Fallon's] house at New Rochelle landing" (I:9).

McDonald's informants occasionally do not know to which side (which "party") an irregular belonged; danger was everywhere. People could be shot with little provocation, and the houses of the innocent burned to the ground in order to flush out those who were hiding inside. Townspeople were at war with neighbors, if they knew with which side their neighbors sympathized. Many of the combatants were not professional soldiers, and so they often acted for personal reasons; in a small town like New Rochelle those personal reasons could be intensely malicious and could harbor many years of anger and hostility. Neighbor fought neighbor, the English fought against the Continentals (when they could identify them), and they also robbed and shot the French (populous in New Rochelle) and other "foreigners." As with all such civil wars, treachery and deceit were ordinary events. Mrs. ("Madam") Mead recalled that one night a stranger came

> to my fathers who at first refused him admittance, but consented on his saying he should perish if not taken in, and on his complying with my fathers request to hand his gun in through the window, breach foremost. He said to my father who directed him to a bed upstairs: "I hope you will not betray me." He slept late, and my father rose early, and, deeming it his duty, informed the authorities who took him [Barrett]. His execution without judge or jury was generally censured. He was a foreigner—and, I believe, an Irishman. (I:75)

Just another night in the life of the Neutral Ground. A stranger comes to an unknown house one night, and pleads to be allowed to spend the night there, lest he perish. The host agrees, but only after the foreigner gives him his gun. When seeing him to a guest bed, the host hears the further plea that the stranger (welcomed up to this point) hopes that he will not be betrayed; early the next morning the host notifies the authorities, who come to the house and execute the guest summarily. Duty has been served.

Shube Merritt, we have seen, was not liked or respected by his neighbors. Lydia (described succinctly by McDonald as "a colored woman") recounted a time when Shube and two friends came to the house of her master. A French sutler had earlier come to the house to purchase some wine, and while he was in the cellar getting it, Shube and two friends arrived: "Shube shot the Frenchman dead, and, searching him, found a belt around his body filled with gold—one hundred Louis d'ors 'tis said. This was divided among three of them" (I:53).

Samuel Oakley remembered that

> Shube Merritt took Capt. Lockwood prisoner, and not wishing to be troubled with prisoners said, "stand off so many as twenty paces [or run so many paces, I will fire, and if] my gun misses fire you shall go clear!" Merritt's gun missed fire, and Lockwood forthwith escaped. Afterwards Lockwood was patrolling in Rye and he heard that Merritt was in Mamaroneck with a party. He pursued, and Shube Merritt with five others retreated along the shore to a house at New Rochelle landing. Here they were surrounded. They took to the upper story and refused to surrender. Lockwood then exclaimed that they must burn the house. Fire was applied, and when Shube's party felt the smoke they offered to give up on promise of quarter. Quarter was given, but Lockwood then said, "Merritt, you shall have the same quarter you gave me. Go twenty paces, and if I miss, you are clear." Shube ran, Lockwood fired and killed him dead. Shube was a small man from Rye or near there. (I:6-7)

"Reputable historians" may now claim that Cooper exaggerated the Skinners' activities (Grossman 1949, p. 27), but the records of events in the McDonald papers show that if anything he understated them. Whatever Cooper's sources for events in Westchester during the Revolution, he certainly did not need printed models; he had only to hear what had actually happened. The facts were lively and dramatic and violent enough.

12

The Neutral Ground

Many novels, particularly novels of espionage, have a No-Man's-Land, or what Cooper called, following Scott, the Neutral Ground. In such a region one can never be certain of one's friends, and danger lurks everywhere. This danger is all the more lethal because it is hidden, or transformed, or in the guise of friends. Truth is an anomalous concept, and nobody speaks it. The environment is entirely hostile and continually on the verge of violence; yet the inhabitants do not wear uniforms, they have no identifying marks, and their intentions, their loyalties cannot be fathomed. To which side are they really loyal?

As conceived by Cooper, the idea of the Neutral Ground—or No-Man's-Land—has become almost a fixture among espionage novel formulas. The original idea so identifies a specific land area, as was the region between the warring armies' lines during the Revolution. It is here that Harvey Birch operates and has his home. His loyalties are known to a very few. Soldiers in the colonists' army think that he is pro-British, and the British are equally suspicious of him. The Whartons, who live in the Neutral Ground, accept him, but only warily.

The wilds are the natural habitat of Harvey Birch; he is most at home there, most at ease in those regions where most mortals fear to tread. Shunning open spaces, meadows, and built-up areas, Birch cannot be located when he is in the woods and uncharted hills. That is where he takes Henry Wharton when trying to evade rebel soldiers: they observe Birch and his charge disappear into the wilds, but cannot find them once they have gone there. Only Birch knows his way around in these uncharted lands, and he is able to use this knowledge of the wilderness to escape from those pursuers whose knowledge does not exceed the charted ways. The Neutral "Ground" can be a body of water, as it is for those plucky English yachtsmen, Davies and Carruthers, in what is often thought of as the first spy novel, Erskine Childers' *The Riddle of the Sands*. At sea these amateur intelligence agents must conceal the purpose of their explorations from everyone they encounter, even those who appear to be friendly—or politically neutral. A German yacht tries to run them down; shifting tides threaten to strand them offshore. Sandbars appear and in the next tide vanish. Davies becomes romantically interested in a young woman aboard a "mystery yacht": but at sea, beyond the aegis of British law, they must fend for themselves in a world that is full of potential dangers.

The Neutral Ground becomes more ominous as the spy novel develops—and as our world becomes more ominous. World War I revived the term "No-Man's-Land" as a place of desolation and perpetual danger for its inhabitants; it is not merely "neutral." The hero of Grahame Greene's *The Confidential Agent*, "D," experiences a No-Man's-Land in London of the late 1930s, where he is an alien. The people around him live their peaceful, uneventful, quotidian lives; there is nothing remarkable about London to them. It is where they are at home, where little that is extraordinary or dangerous ever happens. But approaching this city by road, "D" is beaten up, and later in town he is shot at. The important papers he is carrying are stolen from him without his knowledge; and the young chambermaid in the hotel where he stays, for whom he develops paternal fondness, is thrown from an upper-story window. The "other side" tries to bribe him, then kill him, in their attempts to bring about the failure of his assignment. Those of his own side do not trust him; and so he must make his way through London evading unforeseen and unseen dangers, all in the name of a cause for which he feels no urgent commitment.

And the No-Man's-Land can be of the agent's mind—as it is in part for "D," who reflects, sadly, that he carries the war, and death, around with him. This is paranoia, for "D" or for any character of fiction who believes that enemies are all around him, and that no one is to be trusted or loved. This extension of the "neutral ground" is an indirect descendant of Cooper's insights.

This region of danger threatens James Bond before he even sails for Dr. No's island fortress. While he is in Jamaica, attempts are made on his life—by dropping poisonous insects onto his sleeping body while he is in bed at night, by booby-trapping his toothpaste, by gunfire directed at him in noisy places, in crowded places. A secret agent in Bond's department has been mysteriously killed—but by whom and for what reason? Crab Key will not be a "No-Man's-Land"; that is sheer, unmistakable danger because that is enemy territory.

No-Man's-Land can be one's own country, or at least an ostensibly friendly country. This is the situation facing John Buchan's South African hero Richard Hannay (in *The Thirty-Nine Steps*), who finds himself on the run (Harvey Birch's perpetual condition) from the members of the German "Black Stone" organization, who hunt him by automobile and airplane, and from the British police, who he thinks are seeking him for the murder of his neighbor. (He didn't do it, and they really aren't after him.) At one point Hannay wanders into the country house of the "Bald Archaeologist" and feels relieved at having eluded his pursuers, but his euphoria lasts just a few minutes, before it is revealed that the archeologist is actually the chief of the "Black Stone." Hannay is taken captive, but makes a hairbreadth escape and eventually brings the plotting Germans to justice.

Or No-Man's-Land can be one's neighborhood, comfortable one minute and fraught with overt and clandestine danger the next. William Goldman's Babe Levy (the "Marathon Man" of the book's title) quickly finds that his familiar Manhattan street is a No-Man's-Land when Szell and his hirelings first mug him in Central Park, then capture him in his apartment, and torture and then try to kill him; when Janeway, who first identifies himself as his brother's colleague, is revealed to be in league with the enemy; when Else, with whom he is infatuated, turns out to be working for his would-be assassins. The corner street gang, from whom in the past he has only received abuse and threats, at a crucial moment comes to his aid. In this No-Man's-Land those who appear to be dangerous can be recruited to render assistance, while nearly all those in whom one trusts—or about whom one is ignorant—are full of murderous intent.

For Le Carré—as for all of us until the fall of 1989—this deadly region of peril and incertitude is at the Berlin Wall. *The Spy Who Came in from the Cold* begins and ends there; in the novel's opening chapter a British agent waits on the American side of "Checkpoint Charley" for one of his sub-agents to cross over to safety from the East. It is night (the only really appropriate time for action in the Neutral Ground) and Leamas stood, waiting, in the dim light of the arclights, in front of him the road and to either side the Wall, a dirty, ugly thing of breeze blocks and strands of barbed wire, lit with cheap yellow light, like the backdrop for a concentration camp. East and west of the Wall lay the unrestored part of Berlin, a half-world of ruin, drawn in two dimensions, crags of war (Le Carré 1983, p. 5).

The setting is right for an ignominious death, and soon the agent whom Leamas is awaiting will die trying to cross through the checkpoint.

The Wall, this contemporary No-Man's-Land, is a powerful symbol of death. For one thing, people die there: in this novel the victims are Riemeck, Liz, and Leamas, all of whom are shot while trying to cross over or through it. The Wall—before October 1989—was flanked by devices of death—land mines, barbed wire, steel and concrete tank traps. It was patrolled by armed guards on foot with their trained dogs, while above them more guards, armed, manned machine guns in watch towers. Moving away from the Wall does not ensure safety, either; the agents of one side (in this novel the East Germans) move into the territory of the other to accomplish an occasional assassination. All of Berlin is to some degree infected with this murderous contagion. Further away, away from this dangerous city and its murderous Wall, lies relative safety. Away from the Wall people may live quotidian lives, and die only from accident, disease, civilian crime, and aging.

James Thorpe has suggested to me that America does have a Neutral Ground today: the Bronx, New York. Perhaps this is only the misperception of an out-of-towner (from California); perhaps. However, undeniably, the Bronx is a region of "drive-by" shootings, frequent cabbie muggings, random killings and rapes, gun-fights between opposing sides in drug wars, shootings in which the innocent are often killed by accident. Everyone, seemingly, is armed. In this multi-ethnic community nearly all are ostensibly Americans but many have other ethnic accents and dress styles. The neutrals, the hostiles, narcotics agents in disguise, all are hardly visible, and then only to the experienced, and even they are often wrong. The cops, perhaps no more criminal than other American police forces, are frequently enough thought to be, and in fact found to be, taking bribes. Many cabs won't pick up or deliver passengers to certain areas in the Bronx, especially at night. Crime in the subways may be overestimated by the public, but the popular perception is that they are very dangerous places. One does not know whom to trust, if anyone. The most innocuous-seeming are murderous. "Subway Vigilante" Bernhardt Goetz had had enough when he shot four alleged assailants (in Manhattan), and his act was widely applauded by the New York public. Away from the Bronx, from the danger zone's center, one's perception is of less frequent crime; dangerous still, but less so. In the minds of many this is America's neutral zone today.

The spy must conceal his intentions, plans, beliefs, and so on. The spy's essential invisibility enables him to move freely, and to gather whatever information he chooses, but his intentions must necessarily remain hidden, or else the British would imprison Birch and his function as intelligence gatherer would end. Birch's real intentions are known only to "Harper," and that causes the peddler difficulty; for while he must live in one world—that of the society around him—he clandestinely exists in quite another. One life is heartfelt, is true to feelings and ideas and inclinations which are part of his constitution, the other an adopted mode of existence meant to deceive all those around him. His is a life continually on the alert. Yet without this dual existence he would be ineffective, as Cooper saw nearly two centuries ago.

Again we turn to John Le Carré for the most articulate expression of this aspect of the clandestine life. British agent

Alec Leamas is talking to his interrogator, Fielder, who interrupts his questioning to declaim on the necessary loneliness of their lives:

> In itself, the practice of deception is not particularly exacting; it is a matter of experience, of professional *expertise*, it is a facility most of us can acquire. But while a confidence trickster, a play-actor or gambler can return from his performance to the ranks of his admirers, the secret agent enjoys no such relief. For him, deception is first a matter of self-defense. He must protect himself not only from without but from within, and against the most natural of impulses: though he earn a fortune, his role may forbid him the purchase of a razor; though he be erudite, it can befall him to mumble nothing but banalities; though he be an affectionate husband and father, he must under all circumstances withhold himself from those in whom he should naturally confide. (Le Carré 1983, p. 125)

It is a small step to the spy's essential vulnerability; Cooper saw this also. The spy must appear to have one set of beliefs, convictions, and intentions to many with whom he lives and associates, and cannot reveal his true intentions, yet must remain in good stead with those he does not necessarily like or admire, thus exposing himself to danger and the hostility from those who misunderstand him.

Because of the animus against the spy as literary hero—or hero of any stamp—writers subsequent to Cooper neglected his insights, and allowed the spy novel to lie fallow. In any event, Harvey Birch is less on the page, less a hero than Henry Wharton, Dunwoodie, even Harper (Washington). Birch is not the stuff of which romantic, fictional heroes are made, and was thus a source of imitation for an occasional dime novel only. Such was L. A. Jones' *The Wooden-Legged Spy* (1909).

Buchan's first fictions did not invent the character of the spy-hero, that development having been prepared for by certain "imaginary war" novels and fictions (and docu-fictions such as were written by William Le Queux). Dime novels such as the *Wooden-Legged Spy* exerted no influence. By Buchan's time the animus against the spy in literature could be overcome by making him a private citizen, not an agent, who acted out of patriotism. The first heroes of espionage fictions were amateurs and gentlemen, and they acted primarily as ad hoc counterespionage agents: Hannay, Carruthers and Davies, Ashenden.

Cooper's *The Spy* gradually languished as interest in André waned; the role of the spy was not an appropriate one for a hero, and his potential as symbol could not be realized in a societal structure whose bureaucratic organization had not yet developed oppressively.

Then, by luck, the fortunes of the spy of fiction changed. Espionage became a major weapon of the military and naval arsenals, and spies came to public attention—and not always in a negative way. British intelligence officers intercepted a German diplomatic coded message, and with what became known as the Zimmerman Telegram persuaded President Wilson of hostile German intentions. The OSS sent agents into Germany to help defeat Hitler. If they were caught and executed, they became instant heroes. And as life in the West became increasingly bureaucratic and compartmentalized, the idea of the spy, and his putative ability to spy on others to whom one normally did not have access, gained attractiveness.

Cooper could not have foreseen these developments. He could not have known of the elevation of the spy's social standing or of the existence, let alone the mushrooming of professional espionage agencies. Nothing in his writing suggests that he anticipated the emergence of such highly specialized, compartmentalized social structures. So it is by chance that his insights of 1820 have relevance to the twentieth century. Those insights had to be reinvented by other writers when the times were right—that is, when the times made such perceptions relevant—for such reinventions. Cooper's visions were in the wrong era, and so we cannot really call them insights, when he had no accurate "vision" of his reality. Accidents of history and cultural evolution have made a prophet of him.

Grossman criticizes Cooper's looseness and his slovenliness throughout his writing career (1949, p. 28). But Grossman concedes, at times, "on great occasions, especially in his early work," the reader may wonder if Cooper really knew what he was doing. One of the arguments of this book is that he probably did—a good deal of the time. And whether he did or not seems secondary to the fact of his achievement—generic, and psychologically perspicacious as they are. One can only speculate how much of it was done by accident, how much the outcome of subsequent history (and subsequent literary history) which he could not have foreseen, has made his reputation and his contributions to American letters.

Part Three

THE SPY

13

An American Novel

Cooper had begun writing *The Spy* before he was working on his first novel, *Precaution*, but the work went slowly. It was to be his first "American" novel, and so it was important to him; he intended to answer, implicitly, Sidney Smith's famous challenging question, "In the four quarters of the globe, who reads an American book?" Cooper was very conscious of the challenge implied in Smith's rhetorical query; he had thoroughly interiorized it. From early childhood, Cooper was aware of Americans' diffidence when confronted with all things British, and his countrymen's love for many aspects of British culture, especially literature, politics, and morals (Grossman 1949, p. 14). He was himself diffident about writing this American novel, and uncertain about the project. Then, in the fall of 1820 Cooper put *The Spy* aside as being "too great a financial risk" (Wallace 1986, p. 85).

Writing an American novel—about American subjects, set in America, peopled with Americans—was going to be an especially difficult task for him for several reasons: the literary ground was uncharted, American scenes and characters were too familiar to his countrymen, and their familiarity with subject and background would evoke their contempt of his efforts; or so he feared. If Cooper was going to make any factual mistakes in this novel, his audience would immediately know it. Patriotism in those early days just after the Revolution often amounted to little more than financial concern; and he was reluctant to compete with fellow countryman James Brockton Brown (Wallace 1986, p. 87). As he wrote in the preface to the first edition of *The Spy*, "There are several reasons why an American, who writes a novel, should choose his own country for the scene of his story—and there are more against it." An American author is better able to delineate character and to describe scenes when he is familiar with both of them. Additionally, Cooper felt, "the ground is untrodden, and has the charms of novelty" (1821, p. v). Despite his doubts, Cooper was hopeful of the book's eventual financial success: after all, only one other writer had ever done this kind of project, and he was now dead. Cooper's book's novelty was thus enhanced, and "gives the book some small chance of being noticed abroad, since our literature is much like our wine—it benefits by traveling." A final reason: "the patriotic ardor of the country will ensure a sale" (1821, p. v).

At bottom, he thought, his intimacy with things American was an advantage, even though American scenes lacked certain anticipated romantic appurtenances, especially castles and lords. Cooper explains, redundantly, that the book will have none of these things because the country has none (I, p. x). He relates that he had searched among his acquaintances for an authentic nobleman; but when he found one, a female acquaintance "wouldn't have him if he were a king" (I, p. xi). He traveled to "a renowned castle" one hundred miles to the east, but it had so many broken windows, and was such "an out-door kind of place," that he could not imagine placing any family in it during cold weather. And so he has to invent anew, so he says, characters and sites (I, p. xi). Authenticity weighs on his mind; and while he cannot "absolutely aver that the whole of our tale is true," he honestly believes that "a good portion of it is" (I, p. xi). Close enough.

Sir Walter Scott's influence is noticeable throughout this second effort. Railton (1978, p. 63) simply states as fact, without bothering to support his claim, that *The Spy* was influenced by Scott's historical novels. The claim has been, of course, unchallenged. The idea of the "Neutral Ground" can be found in several of Scott's tales, though in America this ground is more akin to a variant of a No-Man's-Land; the Revolutionary War version is that terrain where the regular armies fought during the day, and where irregulars of both sides, privateers without transcendent loyalties, skirmished and pillaged at night (Wallace 1986, pp. 89, 93).

He liked *The Spy*, even before it was finished, but he was nevertheless fearful, in advance, of a negative public reaction. In retrospect, it is hard to see why. The book dealt with a glorious era of American history, it extolled the American character and patriotism, and the character of Washington (a.k.a. Harper in the novel) was drawn with a "quasireligious aura" (Wallace 1986, p. 92). His worry was proven groundless; the novel sold very well, was the first American novel to be a best seller, its sales aided no doubt by the burst of patriotism evoked by the recently concluded War of 1812 (Wallace 1986, pp. 108-109). This war replicated the Revolution, stirring similar chauvinist passions.

Nevertheless, Cooper fretted about its critical reception—especially the opinions of the British critics, whose judgments would be enormous in the decision of many Americans whether to buy—and read—the book or not. British critics exercised that enormous a control over any English-language novel's fate, copies of which they would themselves read in pirated editions. But until they passed judgment, an American author could not know whether he had succeeded or failed. Happily, they gave *The Spy* thumbs up. American reviewers, more cautious about homemade products, praised it with a mild casualness, or were noncommittal (Grossman 1949, p. 28). Although Cooper would at a subsequent time claim not to be interested in popularity—"If I were anxious for popularity I should cut my throat in despair"—in the Preface to *The Pioneers* he allowed that *The Spy* "was written to see if I could not overcome this neglect of the reading world" *(Precaution* had not sold well) (quoted in Railton 1978, p. 32).

The critics had some reservations about the character of Colonel Wellmere, of course, but in general they approved of Cooper's narrative, though some of them quibbled that the book's denouement seemed rushed (Railton 1978, p. 21). It was in Cooper's introduction for a later edition that he spelled out the compositional and editorial process that had caused this admitted awkwardness: as the second volume grew in length, the publisher worried lest the expense of printing eat up the projected profits. So, to put him at his ease on this matter, Cooper wrote the last chapter (which was printed and paged) "before the chapters which precede it were even thought of" (quoted in Railton 1978, p. 21). Nevertheless, as we now know, the book was a great success and was eventually translated into a number of European languages: French, German, Spanish, and Italian of course; but also into Russian, Swedish, and Danish (Grossman 1949, pp. 28-29).

Since the story of André was already something of "an American folk epic" (Pickering 1971, p. 22), Cooper could be sure that his carefully planted echoes of and allusions to the André affair would strike "at once a sympathetic chord in his American readers" (ibid.). Leisy (1929, p. 6) thought that Cooper must have been delighted with the possibilities of his subject, owing to the great public interest in the fates of Nathan Hale and of André. A New York-produced play by Cooper's friend, William Dunlap extolling the unfortunate major drew a large crowd to its performance. André's fame grew; all America knew and revered him. When he was reintered, the peach tree which had subsequently grown over André's grave was carefully removed as well, for replanting in one of the king's gardens. The major's remains were reburied in the south aisle of Westminster Abbey, and a monument erected there to his honor and remembrance.

In June and July of 1821 the New York *Evening Post* published stories about the Arnold/André conspiracy, treason, and execution. The articles did not indicate that the newspaper knew of André's imminent reinterment in Westminster chapel; nevertheless, "apparently without advance publicity" (Decker 1959, p. 119), a British warship arrived in New York in August 1821, and then sailed up the Hudson to Dobbs Ferry on 10 August. *The Evening Post* did not think the event newsworthy enough to cover the story of the *Phaeton's* arrival and mission. Three days later, however, it did publish an account of the ceremony, given them by an unidentified eyewitness. André's remains were respectfully placed in a mahogany sarcophagus, and that in turn subsequently placed on board the *Phaeton*.

Cooper's narrative was wound around a political and familial conflict, interspersed with the patriotism of the new republic; the primary means for energizing this thematic matrix was the character of Harvey Birch. He was created as a socially marginal character, as was the alleged model in John Jay's anecdotes that Cooper is said to have used (Wallace 1986, pp. 100-101). Cooper is not helpful on the matter of his sources: "we do not absolutely aver," he wrote in the preface to the 1821 edition of *The Spy* (I, p. xi), "that the whole of our tale is true; but we honestly believe that a good portion of it is." It would have been inappropriate, according to the aesthetic conventions of the time, to have had any of the Whartons, or the people who frequented their home, be the spy. In reviewing the book, Maria Edgeworth (writing to *Port Folio* 1823, p. 68) said that "neither poetry nor prose can ever make a spy an heroic character. From Dolon in the Iliad to Major André, and from Major André to this instrument of Washington, it has been found impracticable to raise a spy into a hero. Even the punishment of hanging goes against all heroic stomachs—the scaffold is a glorious thing, and may be brought on the stage with safety—but would even Shakespeare venture the gibbet?"

Birch was not the stuff of which early nineteenth century heroes were made—but more, much more, of that later. He is, as already noted, a socially marginal character, landless, with no reputable occupation, without socially prominent friends, a man of disguises with no certifiable identity, seemingly acquisitive. During the course of the novel, Birch loses everything of material value: his metal chest which contains his gold hoard, his house, then his freedom of movement (which is essential for the spy), and finally (though only temporarily) even his reputation as an honest peddler. Cooper makes him acceptable to the reader by making him a valiant patriot (a commitment to country that the novel's characters are ignorant of), impressively a penniless patriot who refuses to accept gold when it is offered him for payment.

Several historical prototypes for Birch have been suggested (there are none in literature), but none has been entirely convincing. Most likely Cooper never learned from John Jay's lips the name of his agent; but legends about spies were widely current lore of the "Neutral Ground" (Pickering 1971, p. 24) and Cooper would have found it difficult to avoid hearing such tales.

One particular spy, never mentioned as a Birch prototype—and with good reason—was the British agent Ann Bates. She worked for the "other" side, was a woman, and less importantly, in normal times she was a Philadelphia school teacher. She knew first hand something of West Chester's wilderness. Much of her field work was in the area north of New York City, including the Neutral Ground. On one mission she traveled to several encampments of the rebel army, making several contacts on her own initiative. She was married to a British army armorer, and so knew something about weapons: their caliber, their weight, range, and so on. At each Continental encampment that she visited she made a professionally detailed note of the armament, marking "the strength and situation of each brigade and the number of cannon, with their situation and weight of ball" (Hatch 1986, p. 157). On another mission she was even able to penetrate Washington's headquarters, where she picked up military information from an unsuspecting aide.

At one large encampment she ran into an acquaintance who, possibly because he was a Freemason, she felt that she could trust. She was pathetically underpaid by her British controls, but she gave her Freemason contact what money she could from her peddling profits. For his small wages the agent contacted other Freemasons, strategically placed within the rebel commissary department, and that information was given to her and then passed on to Sir Henry Clinton's intelligence officers in New York. Passing through the Neutral Ground on her way back to safe ground, she was stopped, strip-searched, and robbed, by rebels. Her superior officer, André could have learned espionage tradecraft from her; she carried no incriminating papers with her, having committed all her intelligence information to memory, and the American guards thus found nothing of military value in her belongings.

She served both Captains Robert Donkin and (later Major) John André, and served them both well. Although for persuasive reasons Ann Bates was not Cooper's model for Birch, she is worth mentioning here because of the coincidence that she, like Harvey, was able to go from camp to camp, from brigade to brigade, disguised as an itinerant peddler.

But Cooper was not a proto-feminist, and *The Spy* does not acknowledge the role that women played in the war, however invisible that role. It is a novel which turns over and over the idea of disguise and the act of spying, and women were not a part of that world. Only innocent Frances comes close. Several people are in disguise in this novel; not only Harvey Birch—whose intentions are concealed rather than his appearance—but Washington as well, as the mysterious stranger "Harper." Captain Henry Wharton is a disguised British officer who has used his deception to get him past the American lines, though he is in the midst of the Neutral Ground while he is at home. In this as in other respects Cooper made his situation similar to that of André's. Wharton has made use of a forged pass; he also is captured in a compromising position, tried by a military tribunal, and sentenced to death according to the "usages of war." Pickering (1971) remarks that the parallel is both "unmistakable and deliberate" (p. 22). Cooper places the first days of the novel at the end of October 1780, only days after the real André had been captured and hanged.

The Spy marks the first appearance of a number of stock characters of American fiction for more than a century to come: the Yankee peddler, the American Negro servant (the first of a long line of faithful, comic Negroes in American literature), the dashing cavalryman (Pickering 1971, p. 23). The characters of high social station are less interesting—a Cooper trademark—than those of the low (Grossman 1949, p. 25). Yet they are not aristocrats, but members of the middle class; the servants and working class people are, Harvey Birch excepted, usually merely comic cardboard outlines. Cooper's sketching of women, for better or worse, would be an American fictional standard for more than a century. The Wharton girls are fair or have light brown hair; they are extremely sensitive and delicate, virtuous (of course), their passions refined and tamed. Those with dark hair are passionately tempestuous, wildly seductive, a danger to a society that values in its relationships a controlled and ordered hierarchy.

14

Dramatis Personae

HARVEY BIRCH

Cooper tells us, so we may better understand his character, that Harvey had been a "pedlar" from his youth; "at least," Cooper cautions us, "so he frequently asserted" (I, 31); he is of humble origin, necessarily, because no gentleman could be a spy. Washington is not a clandestine agent, he is only temporarily in disguise, assumed so that he may communicate with his operatives. We learn that Birch was "supposed" to be a native of one of the Eastern colonies, which validates his character. His father is known to have "something of superior intelligence," which translates into the presumption that in the "land of their nativity" they had known better fortunes. The dull or the stupid would not, in this just cosmos, be prosperous. But Harvey's manners were of the men of his class; he stood apart from them, if at all, only by his acuteness and by the mystery that surrounded his movements (I, 31). Father and son lived in the "humble dwelling" where Washington had at first, reluctantly, sought shelter.

In his peddler role, Harvey is sometimes thought to be a driver of sharp bargains, greedy for profits (a harsh appraisal of Grossman's): appearances are important here; Cooper says that "to a superficial observer, avarice would seem his ruling passion" (I, 35). At the beginning of the revolution he "appeared" to be absorbed in "the one grand object of amassing money" (I, 33). Yet when we first meet him at the Locusts, he is quite willing to be bargained down from an initial (high) asking price by Caesar, the black servant (I, 39).

And when, after his father's funeral, he tries to sell his home, the "speculator" who offers to buy it has no qualms about lowering the offering price after all but the final papers have been drawn up. Harvey agrees, though feeling himself defrauded (I, 222). This is no hard bargainer. From the Continental's perspective, he was, more simply, a dealer in immoral trade with the British.

But his clandestine life—rife with "dark and threatening" hints—soon drew the notice of the authorities, and he came under their scrutiny (I, 33). He was frequently arrested, though never held for long, and he became skilled in escape (I, 34). He is literature's first spy, after all; and Cooper could not resist describing him in terms his readers could not mistake: his gray eyes were sunken and restless, continually flitting, yet when they concentrated on another's face, they "seemed to read the very soul" (I, 34). In conversations about business, about "traffic," his expression was abstracted and restless; but when he spoke about the Revolution, and the new America, "all his faculties were concentrated" (I, 35).

St. Armand thinks that Harvey is modeled on the popular conception of the "Wandering Jew." In a persuasively argued essay (1978, 348-68), he compares Cooper's portrait with several contemporary conceptions of Ahasuerus (as he is sometimes named), the man who for various sinister reasons mocked the Savior as he carried his crucifix to Golgotha—or in variants of the legend, actually scourged Christ himself. Eternal wandering is his punishment. Schiller's portrait, available in English in 1795, is cited (352-53): "Never in my life had I seen a face of such varying expression and of so elusive a character, so much attractive good-nature paired with repellent coldness. In it every passion seemed to have raged and again to have forsaken it." Is Harvey the Ahasuerus of the Neutral Ground? Possibly. But that source for Cooper's conception does not seem to alter the fact of Harvey's role as double agent; it does seem to detract from his innate nobility. If we are reminded of the Wandering Jew, what will we think of him?

Rather, I think that Cooper may not have felt secure in inventing entirely anew a character of such habits—and habitats, a creature of wild and untrodden ways. And so he borrowed elements of character and description from the one denizen of the wilderness of whose description he was sure, and made of him an updated (1821) "Flying Dutchman/Wandering Jew" analog. Harvey is a mysterious resident of the wilds, of uncontrolled nature, though with a heart of gold. So is (was?) the Wandering Jew a figure of mystery; could Cooper have described them in noticeably variant terms? If we see in Harvey Birch any Satanic aspects— Katy suspected that he might be Beelzebub himself—then we lose sight of an important aspect of Birch's character. Let Katy have her superstitious fears; we have to know better, we must have a more sophisticated interpretation of Harvey.

Cooper has made him an effective agent: perceptive, observant, decisive, always in control. In his initial appearance at the Locusts, he is questioned about the progress of the war by the Wharton sisters and then by their father. To each question he gives an ambiguous reply: "it is thought," "I believe that they think so," "people will talk," and so on. To Harper's query about a "probability of movements below" (I, 39), his answer is quite specific: "it is some time since the rig'lar cavalry were out, and I saw some of De Lancey's men cleaning their arms as I passed their quarters; it would be no wonder if they took the scent soon, for the Virginia horse are low in the country" (I, 39). He has given Harper/Washington a description of the quality of the enemy, its character and capability (cavalry), the state of its preparedness, their commander (and the additional information that such knowledge would imply), and he has authenticated his information with the observation that he had seen it all himself.

When all the Whartons behold the distant Hudson and its valley newly bathed in sun, most see nothing noteworthy; Henry sees only spots. Birch identifies those spots as "rig'lars"; there are specifically ten whaleboats, and they would not move so fast "unless they were better manned than common" (I, 56). An astute observer, Birch gives the number of the enemy, their mode of conveyance, and makes an intelligent estimate of their quality: they are regulars. He further estimates that fighting will accompany them. This is spoken in the hearing of Harper, who does not need further intelligence; excusing himself from his host, he says that he will avail himself of the sudden clearing of the weather to get on with his business. Harvey has a final cautionary word to Henry Wharton; now that the storm has lifted, the Skinners will become more active. Birch is usually right about such matters. Better that Henry return to his army.

Cooper gives Harvey an accent: "rig'lars," for one example of many, and occasionally his syntax is colloquial. This inelegant speech, uttered by a person of inherent nobility, anticipates the character and the complexity of Natty Bumppo (see St. Armand 1978, 349). The similarities do not end there; most importantly, neither is good enough for the genteel heroine, yet both are clearly favorites of their author (see McDowell 1930, 513-24).

Birch's effectiveness derives, in part, from his ambiguous social standing. After he leaves the Locusts, returns to his home, and then sojourns "northward," the Whartons conjecture among themselves about him, ignorantly, their confusion reflecting that of the novel's society at large, much to Harvey's advantage. How is it that he can travel freely in these difficult times, Aunt Peyton asks. Henry doesn't know why the "rebels" allow him such liberties, but—he says—Sir Henry (Clinton) protects him. Will he betray you, Henry's father asks; no, thinks Henry, in matters of business he is faithful and reliable. Sarah offers the opinion that Harvey has loyalty, and that is a "cardinal virtue." Henry's rebuttal: "love of money is a stronger passion than love to his king" (I, 62). The Americans are firmly convinced that Harvey is working for the British; when Captain Lawton visits the Locusts and inquires of the peddler, he is told that he is away from home; Lawton responds with the boast that he will someday catch him and hang him—from a birch tree. After having helped Henry escape to a British frigate, Harvey and an accompanying Skinner are stopped by a patrol of Cow-boys; their leader's first question is fatuous, yet nevertheless reveals the peddler's ambiguous appearance and status: "has Washington sent you down as spies?" No, Harvey replies, obviously enough, "I am an innocent pedlar" (II, 251). Birch's purpose, his mission, his deepest personal and political commitments, his character—all of these remain a mystery to everyone. Harvey's ultimate reward must be an inner, and unrecognized, knowledge of the cause he faithfully serves.

No guard, no prison cell can hold him for long. Captain Lawton is particularly incensed against Birch because he had earlier been entrusted to guard him after he had been taken prisoner. Two sentries had been assigned to secure him. A woman, "busily engaged in the employments of the household" (I, 75), had been seen nearby; after Birch had escaped, undetected, the woman had disappeared, and only Harvey's empty knapsack was found in his cell (II, 74-75). Earlier, after yet another arrest, on the morning of his intended execution, "the cage was opened, and the bird had flown" (I, 149). The guards had been hand-picked, and immune to bribery and treason; so how did this peddler do it? After another one of his astonishing escapes, Major Dunwoodie wanted to inquire into it "closely"; the only opening in his cell was its door, and the sentry posted there had seen nothing suspicious (II, 29). The close inquiry revealed that Harvey escaped in woman's clothing—borrowed from the sleeping Betty Flanagan, in whose remaining clothes he left a guinea. When he takes from the poor, he gives to the poor.

Legends developed among the guard details that Harvey had "dealings" with "the dark one" (I, 150). For Sergeant Hollister, Harvey is "the evil-one," "Beelzebub" himself, only disguised as a peddler, and the creatures who appeared to be the Skinners were his "imps" (II, 31). (In folklore, commerce with the "dark one" would be consistent with Birch's burying his gold in the ground). Frances sees him accidentally, and then she is not sure it is him. In the Highlands while the family is leaving the Locusts, the clouds suddenly part, giving her a brief glimpse "into the secrets of that desart [sic] place," where she saw an apparently human figure, "of singular mould and unusual deformity" (II, 141). His captors never learn; Harvey inevitably escapes from them, in disguise or in his own garb, no matter the cell or the guard, and that is always done quickly.

And like the man of shadows of melodrama—he was on the move at those "hours which others allotted to repose." He might be seen near the Highlands and sometime later near the Harlaem River, always on the move, his backpack his sole companion. Outsider's glances at him were "uncertain and fleeting"; between dusk and dawn he could not be followed, or traced, or even seen. He disappeared for months on end, "and no traces of his course were ever known." Sentries posted in the mountains often reported "a strange figure that had been seen gliding by them in the mists of the evening" (I, 149). He was seldom at home; after his father died, he sold the cabin at a desperately low price, gave most of the money to Katy, and assured her that as for his own shelter, "Providence will provide me with a home" (I, 222).

Spying was a dangerous business even then—maybe particularly then. When Katy and Frances talked about contemporary politics, and spying, Katy mentioned "Ondree" who "was hung acrost the Tappaan," and that Harvey's father "was near hand to going crazy about it, and didn't sleep for night nor day `till Harvey got back" (II, 139). If André could be hanged for his deceptions, why not the far less important Harvey Birch? We should not let his successes allow us to forget that basic fact of a spy's life; Cooper didn't.

The ubiquitous man of many guises, and almost as many locations, Harvey appears from nowhere with messages of vital import. Discussion of the capture of the disguised Henry Wharton was interrupted by the sudden appearance of "a small ragged boy" (I, 86) with a barely legible message for Major Dunwoodie: "The rig'lars are at hand, horse and foot." Thus alerted, Dunwoodie and his men mounted and rode off to battle. At battle's end he sought his home in the gathering dusk. Having avoided the retreating English, Birch was seen by Captain Lawton and Lieutenant Tom Mason, who shouted to their men to take the peddler dead or alive. When Birch ran near a convenient wood, horsemen cut off his escape. Intuitively, deceptively, surprisingly, he reversed his course, happily found a convenient wall, and made his escape over it; the horses of the pursuing cavalry would not risk the jump in the dark; the denouement of this chase scene has Captain Lawton across the wall about to sabre Harvey as he lies on the ground, when his horse trips over him, sending both beast and rider to the earth. Harvey emerged from this fumbling with Lawton's sword in his own hands, and so escaped the rebel nooses again; close call for him, near miss for the Americans (I, 136-39).

Harvey saves the day—and Sarah's honor—when he walks into the midst of her wedding ceremony and asks Colonel Wellmere if he can afford to waste any time now that his wife is at that moment in New York harbor, having just arrived from England. The revelation of the scoundrel Wellmere's duplicity sends Sarah into a faint and the onlookers into momentary shock. It is one of Cooper's most melodramatic moments, a hardly believable scene; how did Birch learn of the affair? His exposure of Wellmere's bigamous intentions establishes him solidly on the side of the righteous. And the humble; while all is in confusion, he disappears "with a rapidity that would have baffled pursuit" (II, 80).

His skill as a secret agent aside, Harvey's moral values are important to this novel, possibly more important now than when Cooper wrote it. We understand that Birch could not be the hero of this narrative, given the prevailing attitude toward romantic heroes of fiction of the early nineteenth century. Which makes Harvey a hero of what century? By profession he is an itinerant peddler, hardly a romantic posture. He is suspiciously evasive: the Americans want to catch (and hang) him, his whereabouts are often unknown, he lives in a modest cabin apart from other dwellings, people are never quite sure what to make of Harvey Birch. Katy Haynes, who has been his housekeeper for years, has "never known whether he belonged above or below." He is a man "that no calculation can be made on" (II, 139). Captain Jack Lawton, however, an impetuous, nonrational man of boldness and decision, is unequivocal about Harvey: "the renowned pedlar-spy" he calls him (I, 217). To everyone in the novel, and to many critics, he seems greedy and self-aggrandizing. People watched him closely, when they could, but decided that "his only purpose was the accumulation of gold" (I, 149). But we know, from his last encounter with Harper/Washington, that he refuses a reward of gold. Napoleon once said that the only reward for a spy was gold. Birch gives the lie to that dictum; his reward is the satisfaction of knowing that he has fulfilled his patriotic duty. It is an interiorized reward; no one, especially none of his doubters, will ever know the truth of his inner convictions. Only Washington can appreciate and admire them.

Yet it is a life that has its sorrows, and Harvey has his regrets. We cannot be sure what Cooper had in mind when he showed an occasional vulnerability in him, but Harvey's solitary complaints make him more believable and more sympathetic to us. He complains to Katy shortly after his father has died, and he has sold his house, loosing himself upon the mercies of the world. He will miss his father acutely; while the old man lived, he alone could read the peddler's heart; "what a consolation to return from my secret marches of danger, and the insult and wrong that I suffered, to receive his blessing and his praise" (I, 223).

Astute of Cooper to give the reader this insight into the vulnerability of the man whom all of the characters in the novel think impermeable. Harvey is at bottom humanly susceptible, not an automated espionage machine. He is a spy who can sustain the suspicions and the hostility of those around him, but who nevertheless seeks—from his father— justification and validation. Not even Washington's approbation will suffice; for now that his father is dead, "who is there to do me justice? ... Oh! it is dreadful to die and leave such a name behind me" (I, 223-24). Is this the moment Grossman refers to when he complains that Harvey chooses the moment of his greatest danger to lament the longest about his misunderstood life?—a literary convention which now only survives in opera (Grossman 1949, p. 27). Harvey may not know that it is a moment of greatest danger; and if he does, his indifference to it shows how little he values his own life now that his father—the one person who has understood him—is gone. Shortly after he confronts Dunwoodie at the edge of the woods—where the latter has wandered, aimlessly and thoughtlessly. The peddler levels his musket at the unarmed major, then reveals that he will neither capture nor kill the defenseless officer; what Harvey wants is Dunwoodie's "good opinion ... I wish all good men to judge me with lenity" (II, 26). Men's good opinions of him are fleeting; having rescued Sarah from the Locusts' flames, Harvey stumbles into Lawton, who is overcome with appreciation for Harvey's good works. Can you be what you seem, he blurts out. Harvey does not break his cover: "a royal spy." Lawton does the generous thing: "then go, miserable wretch ... either avarice or delusion has lead a noble heart astray" (II, 96-97).

Birch is a man of strong and admirable character, a man of firm inner convictions, a man who has compromised the appearances of his life for his love of his country; he has sacrificed respectability for the sake of his patriotic convictions. He has chosen the right course and he does not swerve from it. Their inherited values may have discouraged Cooper's contemporaries from admiring such a man; it remains for us to reopen the details of his life and to reappraise his merits. Perhaps that's what Grossman meant when he once said that "his [Birch's] life is intended to illustrate the disinterested love of country" (1949, p. 26). Only the satisfaction of having served a just cause sustains the disinterested Birch; he will continue to live his days in the world of shadows. To the end he is the perfect spy. Deception and obfuscation are part of his nature. Yet Cooper never satisfactorily explains why Harvey's reputation was not restored at the end of the war (perhaps because he wrote the final chapter before those preceding it were finished).

Life imitates art. Birch has not been without his admirers, particularly in other cultures; the distance afforded by such an advantage has given others a perspective that we have not enjoyed. So great was his fame as a literary character that the name was taken by a French secret agent (in irony? as a code name?) who also refused financial rewards for his work (Grossman 1949, p. 26).

The published correspondence of Washington reveals his preference for secret agents "who live with the other side; [and] whose local circumstances, without subjecting them to suspicions, give them an opportunity of making observations." And he also wrote of his idea of espionage that "the persons employed must bear the suspicion of being thought inimical, and it is not within their power to assert their innocence, because that would get abroad and destroy the confidence which the enemy puts in them" (both quotations cited in Pickering 1971, p. 23).

The rootlessness of the occupation of peddler and the ambiguous nature of the Neutral Ground are both metaphors for the transition to nationhood from colonial status. Donald Ringe has said nearly as much with his observation that "the physical environment" establishes "the moral and ethical tone that dominates the book" (1962, p. 29). The Neutral Ground is a sea of chaos between civilized continents of order and hierarchy. Harvey Birch must keep his patriotism clandestine; only with his death are his authentic feelings known—and then not by many.

HENRY WHARTON

The storm that has driven Mr. Harper to the Locusts has harried an initially unwelcome second stranger there. When he comes to the Whartons' door he is admitted, but only because of the severity of the storm. Wharton and his family "disliked the appearance of this new visitor excessively." At table, his rude manners were intrusive: he ate greedily with an appetite "which appeared by no means delicate." On tasting the wine he "gave his lips a smack, that resounded through the room" (I, 12). Despite Cooper's identifying hints, this is not Harvey Birch. When Mr. Harper was shown to his evening's quarters, the boorish stranger's red wig, his stooped posture, disappeared. Henry Wharton was at once recognized by the family's servants, and of course by his father and his sisters. His disguise had gotten him through American "lines," for the subversive purpose of seeing his family. Henry is at first fearful lest Mr. Harper betray him; but Caesar, the servant, assures him that Harper is reliable, for he saw him praying to God on his knees, and such a man would not betray an innocent. Only a Skinner would betray a pious child who was honoring his father with a visit (I, 16).

Like André, Henry Wharton has had a commission bought for him "as the regular stepping-stones to preferment" (I, 17). "Most of the higher offices in the colonies, were filled by men who had made arms their profession" (I, 17). Wharton identifies with André; when he questions the efficacy of his disguise, he points out that the Americans have just recently captured the British major, and would love to get their hands on him just now. But, his father exclaims, "you are not a spy—

you are not within rebel, that is, the American lines;—there is nothing here to spy" (I, 27). This important exchange—in which Cooper establishes the moral basis of a spy's culpability (in this case the lack of it)—occurs in the same conversation in which André is first mentioned. The distinctions are important: Henry is not behind enemy lines; and there is nothing (at the Locusts) to spy on. Not guilty. Henry agrees— he is not guilty. But he admits to passing through Continental pickets at White Plains. He is innocent, but how will it appear?

He is soon captured by a detachment of Continental dragoons under the command of Major Dunwoodie. The Whartons believe that he will free Henry, but when the Continental officer learns that Henry has a forged pass, and that he passed the rebel pickets in disguise (as did André), he cannot release his prisoner. The Whartons apply great pressure to him; Frances, his intended, vows that she will marry him immediately if he will only let her brother go—he is innocent, after all—but Dunwoodie cannot, because the capture of André and the revelation of the Arnold treason has made all of the Continental Army wary. After the battle in which Dunwoodie's men defeat the British, the Locusts become the Continental Army's hospital and headquarters. Henry is recaptured. Dunwoodie does not wish to embarrass him by placing him under guard; instead, he asks for a pledge of honor from the British officer that he will not try to escape. Henry replies that "your generous confidence ... will not be abused, even though the gibbet on which your Washington hung André be ready for my own execution" (I, 124). André has become a character in the action of the novel without being present in it. He is an invisible force shaping Cooper's plot, providing his characters with many of their motivations, causing some of their strongest passions.

Later, at Henry's trial (for entering American "lines" in disguise), Cooper compares his plight with that of André's. Young Wharton admits immediately that he has passed American "picquets" in disguise but that he is nevertheless innocent. It was to visit his aging father, he points out, amid expressions of praise by members of the military tribunal for his honesty. But Henry has used a forged pass (André used one signed by Arnold for "Mr. Anderson"), and that counts against him. Did he have no other purpose for his visit? Henry replies that he had none, but his assertions are not entirely believed. The André affair is still too fresh in the court's memories. The verdict is undecided, however, until Frances, on the witness stand, reveals that her brother had been in touch with "their neighbor, the pedlar Birch" (II, 154). Contact with Harvey Birch is the kiss of death. Henry is convicted of being a spy—"artful," "delusive and penetrating, beyond the abilities of any of his class" (II, 154). Henry is (by identification with André) guilty: "indeed, young man, this is a connexion that may prove fatal to you" (II, 15). The verdict is reached, and it is announced that he is sentenced to be hanged the following morning.

Awaiting what he assumes will be his imminent hanging, Henry Wharton acts further the André manqué. He is brave, noble, and generous to all, even forgiving of Washington, who has granted "every indulgence ... that I can ask for." First, he has asked Dunwoodie to be like a son to his aging father, and a loving brother to Sarah and Frances. In contrast, when the condemned man suggested that the best protection for Frances would be for Dunwoodie to marry her, Frances was not so forgiving and loving: in a rebuke to Dunwoodie's affectionate gesture, she snaps that "none can ever be any thing to me, who aid in my brother's destruction" (II, 164-65).

Washington, who privately knows and understands the situation of Birch and the Whartons, cannot pardon Henry himself; but he does order Birch to effect his escape. And the reader knows, halfway through the second volume, that Henry will be saved when Cooper tells us that, after what Henry believes to be his final meeting with his family, Frances sees in the distance a mysterious figure who is, we will soon learn, scouting the positions of the soldiery (II, 172). We know, and she suspects, that it is Harvey. And if so, all will be well. An unknown minister soon appears at the residence, requesting permission to give final solace to the condemned man. Who can deny such a sacred office? Caesar is brought into the room—and again into the plot, and he and Henry change clothes. They flee through the Neutral Ground—Harvey's natural habitat—where the regulars cannot effectively maneuver. Harvey knows his way unerringly through this uncharted land, is "acquainted with every step that led through the mountains" (II, 240). André also began his escape route through the countryside, the Neutral Ground, and Henry, as did the unfortunate major, sought a ship which was supposed to have been in the Hudson River and which would return him to safety. André's, as we know, had withdrawn; Henry's ship is still waiting.

HARPER/WASHINGTON

Washington, in his disguise as Harper—the first character described by the novelist—is an unambiguous expression of Cooper's attitude, and the prevailing upper-class view of social strata, the author's own as well as the lower classes. Middle-class characters predominate morally; they have an inherent worth. Here is a clear depiction of American social structure—and Cooper's self-assigned place within it—in early nineteenth century East Coast society. Harper, the "tall and extremely graceful person, of apparently fifty years of age" (I, 5), mysterious, yet an obviously ennobled stranger, seeks shelter from an impending storm, but only "the inconvenient tenements of the lower order of inhabitants" seem available; these he eschews because he does not think it either politic or safe to dwell within them (I, 1). The storm comes on with increasing violence, and "Harper" decides to seek shelter at "the next dwelling that offered." He soon finds one, a "very humble" structure, at whose door he knocks without dismounting. A woman—a "female of middle age" (I, 3)—responds, but soon sends him on the road half a mile further: it is more suitable for Cooper's aristocrat. The description of Washington at the novel's beginning, Grossman thought, is "much more in the style of the Bonnie Prince than of the commander of the American armies" (1949, p. 25).

Ever the gentleman, Harper astounds the Whartons—his eventual hosts—by declaring that Henry Wharton, then still out of uniform, should resume his normal appearance: "if any apprehensions of me induce Captain Wharton to maintain his disguise, I wish him to be undeceived—had I motives for betraying him, they could not operate under present circumstances" (I, 45-46). He is, after all, a guest in the Wharton house; and he recognizes at once the innocence of Henry's disguise—more innocent than his own.

Later, Washington cannot act by his own authority to save the imprisoned Henry Wharton, but since he has pledged the young man's safety, he resorts to some covert action: he orders Harvey Birch to effect a rescue (Grossman, p. 25). The commanding general had a reputation in his public life for a "rigid inflexibility"; but Aunt "Miss Peyton" held hopes, in part because he was a Virginian, that in his private life he would be different. In his native colony he was known as a "consistent but just and lenient master" (II, 159). So she felt that even though the military tribunal had found Henry guilty of acting as a spy, Washington's lenient mercy would free him. Dunwoodie was astonished when Washington's letter arrived supporting the court's verdict, but wished to defend his chief, however lame that would sound to his friends: "it is the general, and not the man; my life on it" (II, 164). The aunt knew that Henry was innocent, and she ingenuously assumed that he would be exonerated. But Washington has a public posture to maintain; Wharton cannot be set free when André has recently been taken prisoner out of uniform and hanged for a similar offense. Extra-legally, he orders Harvey to effect the innocent British officer's escape—an "illegal" act which accomplishes a morally correct end.

DUNWOODIE—THE HERO

Introduced within pages of our first meeting with the duplicitous Colonel Wellmere, that "fine young man" with smiling countenance, that "tall graceful youth" with dark complexion and dark sparkling eyes, is greeted joyously by the Wharton ladies. From these first lines we know that Cooper wants us to admire him as do Sarah and Frances. Peyton Dunwoodie is just passing through this first scene, functioning only to contrast with Wellmere, and to utter the dramatic urging to Frances to "be true to your country—be American" (I, p. 25). It is an American novel.

Cooper tells us a little later that when the senior Mr. Wharton had been arrested and detained by the British on some minor infraction—an incarceration encouraged by his neighbors, who hoped thereby to acquire some of his land—it was Major Dunwoodie who arranged for Wharton's release. As a result, does Peyton hate the king, Henry asked. No, Frances assured him, he hates no one, and certainly he loves you, Henry.

Major Dunwoodie is technically the hero, almost by default, since he gets to marry Frances, one of the heroines; but he comes alive only at those moments when he is so priggish as to be funny (Grossman 1949, p. 25).

COLONEL WELLMERE—THE VILLAIN

How not to win a maiden's heart: Colonel Wellmere was one of those officers who availed themselves of the Wharton's hospitality, while "expending his wit on the unfortunate Americans"; in time Frances Wharton listened to his sniping with "great suspicion, and some little resentment" (I, 22). This is Cooper's introduction of him, what we learn of him from the first, and while Cooper is not always precise in his delineation of character (though he could handle clichés), our attitude toward Wellmere consistently flows in this channel. At the Whartons' he is embarrassed by Frances' pointed political sarcasm; after Dunwoodie leaves, he shows the spleen he had tried to repress (I, 25). When his command has been defeated in open battle, he whines, "do you call the route of those irregulars and these sluggish Hessians, a deed to boast of?" (I, 103).

After Wellmere had been defeated in battle, Dunwoodie— the despised rebel—found him on the field brooding disconsolately. The American approached him with apologies for his neglect, which courtesy the English officer received with "coolness." He complained to his American captor that he had been taken prisoner when his horse unaccountably stumbled; but Dunwoodie knew better. He had seen one of his own men "ride him down" (I, 126). Alone with his subordinate, Henry Wharton, Wellmere lamented (in Cooper's sarcastic rhetoric) that his capture has been caused by circumstances "absolutely without the control of man" (I, 195). If only he had the opportunity to relive the action, he would thrash the "yankies" soundly. Nevertheless, with only a slight wordless smile at this facile attempt to distort the actual circumstances of his fall, Dunwoodie escorted him back to the surgeon at the Locusts. The wound was slight; yet even when he accepted medical aid, Wellmere was insulting; when Dr. Sitgreaves offered assistance, the Colonel pretended surprise: "there must be some mistake, sir ... it was a surgeon that Major Dunwoodie was to send me, and not an old woman" (I, 128). The wound is so slight that Dr. Sitgreaves was able to treat it with a "piece of sticking plaster" taken from his pocket (I, 129). When the colonel questions this casual treatment, Sitgreaves replies that since the colonel's wound is not more serious, his purpose must be to report himself wounded in his dispatches; he could report that "an old woman dressed your hurts" (I, 129). Recuperating from his slight wound at the Locusts, colonel Wellmere was given his own room. When visited by Dr. Sitgreaves, he announced that he was too ill to get out of bed (I, 181). Sitgreaves described his condition as "a state of free-will ... he is ill, or he is well, as he pleases" (I, 185).

At table he was somewhat slovenly. When Isabella Singleton arrived at the Locusts to nurse her wounded brother, a toast was offered her at dinner. "The health was drank cheerfully by all but colonel Wellmere, who wet his lips, and drew figures on the table with some of the liquor he had spilt." Then he blurted out, rather nastily (to Captain Lawton), "I suppose, sir, this Mr. Dunwoodie will receive promotion in the rebel army, for the advantage my misfortune gave him over my command" (I, 206). The dinner dissolved into incivilities on several sides. The ladies and the senior Wharton excused themselves discreetly. Left alone, the gentlemen guests turned to arguing about politics, specifically the politics of the American Revolution. The rebels, Wellmere insisted, advanced the cause of slavery; "with confidence in his infallibility" he fell back upon the argument that has since become a cliché: "you are putting the tyranny of a mob on the throne of a kind and lenient prince—where is the consistency of your boasted liberty?" (I, 210). To Dr. Sitgreaves' rebuttal—that the Americans wanted the liberty to govern themselves and not to be ruled by people three thousand miles distant, and who share no common political interest with them—Wellmere sneers that "it is opposed to all the opinions and practices of civilized nations" (I, 211). The doctor replies that it is; and the argument drifts to the subject of slavery. Britain detests the practice, the colonel insists; Britain introduced the practice to the States, his antagonist points out. And so the argument, and the chapter, end (I, 212).

The colonel expressed the conventional British view of the André affair. When Henry Wharton escaped from the Locusts—where he was held in captivity—during the confusion of a nearby battle, he galloped into the company of colonel Wellmere. Breathless, he gasped out the narrative of his capture and of his escape, commenting that he had escaped André's fate; "those traitors," the colonel declares, would never dare to commit another murder in cold blood. Is it not enough that they took the life of André?" (I, 102).

Yet Wellmere is able to win a maiden's heart—for a few moments. A hasty proposal was made to Sarah, and accepted. Because of the "unsettled state of the country" (II, 66) the "lovers" decided that another meeting would be uncertain, and that it was prudent to seize the moment. A priest conveniently arrived at the Locusts, apparently to arrange for an exchange of the wounded, but was pressed into performing the nuptial service. Frances was dubious of the whole affair, and fate seemed to support her when Wellmere realized that he did not have a ring; the priest insisted that he would not perform the ceremony without one. Dr. Sitgreaves offered an unused ring from his family legacy, and Caesar was sent for it at the doctor's home. He arrived back at the Locusts with the prized gold; Sarah and Wellmere were roused from their nervous intermission; the priest stepped forward to resume the ceremony—all was finally in order, when Harvey strode boldly into the room, and with a low bow, asked with ironic naïveté, "can Colonel Wellmere waste the precious moments here, when his wife has crossed the ocean to meet him? ... a few hours riding would take him to the city" (II, 80). Sarah fainted dead away, and all around her was astounded confusion. Wellmere blurted out, "'Tis false—'tis false as hell! ... I have ever denied her claim; nor will the laws of my country compel me to acknowledge it" (II, 81). Confusion and chaos; and shortly after, conflagration. But Harvey has saved the day. A little later, he will also save the fainted and delirious Sarah from the flames; all in all, a good night's work. As Cooper begins to tidy up the various strands of his novel, we learn with Dunwoodie and friends that Wellmere has left for home, and the price of his passage has been his reputation: he was "lowered in the estimation of every honest man in the royal army" (II, 269).

Yet at first the Whartons spoke well of him. Henry pointed out to his family that he was "the eldest son of a man of wealth [family lineage was an important matter with Cooper], so handsome, and a colonel" (I, 48). This is part of an only half-serious estimation of his virtues as a husband for Frances. "A very pretty man" she added. This is not a novel of character development, or even of change. Wellmere is constant; the attitudes of those around him slowly develop until they comprehend the truth about him.

SECONDARY VILLAINS: THE SKINNERS

The Skinners, "whose mouths are filled with liberty and equality, and whose hearts are overflowing with cupidity and gall," are the true villains of the novel, according to Grossman (1949, p. 27). When they first assaulted Birch's home, he had just returned to attend to his dying father—who was "all" in the world to him (I, 155). A Skinner appeared at the door, dressed filthily, his mind "long agitated by evil passions" (I, 156). He was a leader of "one of those gangs of marauders who infested the country with a semblance of patriotism, and were guilty of every grade of offense." Behind their leader stood several of his band, whose "countenances expressed nothing more than the callous indifference of brutal insensibility" (I, 157). After they burned Harvey's house, the Skinners attacked the Locusts itself, pillaging its valuables before they set it ablaze; and thus changing the course, and the main location, of the novel. Betty Flanagan made no distinction between

Skinners and Cow-boys: "a thief's a thief ... whether he stales [steals] for King George or for Congress" (II, 109). Critics and historians may now be undecided about the worth and patriotism of the Skinners; Cooper was not. Did he accurately portray these irregulars? Are they included in the novel as devices to vary the tonal voice of the story and to make the patriotic cause more interesting for having included wicked men on its side?

Henry Wharton was warned early in his stay at the Locusts to be cautious of the Skinners; he was disdainful, because a "few guineas will buy off those rascals at any time." Harvey Birch cautioned him that "money could not liberate Major André." Is this ambiguous? Is the meaning in this exchange that the Skinners are incorruptible? Or that they are patriots, as Washington wrote in his official correspondence? Or that they are unpredictable, sometimes bribable, sometimes not, depending on the time, the situation, the particular Skinners? The Wharton sisters argued that Birch was to be heeded in such matters, but Henry was confident in his own abilities. Birch reminded him that his pass would soon expire; "cannot you forge another?" Henry asked (I, 60).

The Skinners captured Harvey during a raid on his house—the "raid" which has burned his house to the earth—and brought him to the reveling Dunwoodie and Lawton for their reward: gold is the expected payment for the capture of this "traitor to [his] country" (I, 247). Lawton led them off to his quarters for their reward; Dunwoodie confronted Birch, reminding him that he had already been tried (in absentia) and convicted of treason. Dunwoodie declared that "even the justice of Washington condemns you"; Birch saw a moment of daylight. "No," he cried, "Washington can see beyond the hollow views of pretended patriots" (I, 249). He reached for a tin box within the folds of his shirt—it contained the document that could save him—but after a moment's hesitation replaced it: "it dies with me" (I, 250).

Meanwhile, the Skinners' leader was not content with his gold reward; when out of earshot of the soldiers, he suggested to captain Lawton that if given the protection of dragoons, he and his men could "do many an important piece of service" and that "it could be made profitable to the officer" (II, 13). The

Skinner pushed his luck too far; didn't the captain think that Paulding's party (the capturers of André) were "fools" for not letting their man escape? Lawton replied that they were fools indeed; King George would have paid them more handsomely (II, 15-16). Lawton's sarcasm was finally apparent, even to the Skinner; at the last, he inquired again about his reward and Lawton, contemptuously, threw a bag of guineas at his feet (II, 16). But justice is as concrete as it is moral; no sooner had Lawton rewarded the Skinners than he charged them with "burning, robbing and murdering," had them stripped by the guards nearby, and each given the "Law of Moses—forty save one" (II, 17). The only good Skinner ...

Having seen Henry safely off to one of his navy's frigates, Harvey and an unwelcome Skinner were surrounded on the road by a patrol of Cow-boys. Birch had a valid pass, and the irregulars released him. But not the Skinner; for several whimsical reasons, for no particular reason, from a convenient nearby barn rafter they summarily hanged him.

FRANCES

Many people spy in *The Spy*. Walking in the woods after her brother's sentencing, Frances thought that she spied Harvey, and she set out after him. She found instead a small cabin in the wilds and, expecting to find Harvey and her brother inside, stole up beside it and peered within. She too thus became, in the morality of the day, a kind of spy. She was both disappointed, as Henry was not there, and surprised to see the athletic, handsome form of Harper. Frances could not control herself, and burst in upon him, throwing herself at his knees, pleading for him to save her brother's life. For Harper the game was momentarily up; admitting that he was more than Harper, Washington assured her that at that very moment Birch and her brother were on their way to the cabin, and from thence her sibling will be shown back to his own lines (II, 221-23).

CAESAR

Even he is involved, though superficially, in spying. Cooper says of him that early in Harper's visit to the Locusts he had heard low murmuring issuing from the stranger's bedroom (he was presumably getting information from and giving instructions to Harvey Birch). In Cooper's rhetoric, Caesar "had established a regular system of espionage," though only for an innocent cause— the safety of his young master (I, 53).

He is less of an "agent," more an astute observer, when he is told that his mistress is about to be married. The news comes as no surprise to him, because he has seen Sarah and Wellmere talking together, alone, and he has guessed their plans (II, 66). Innocent in spirit and in action, Caesar's "spying" is the innocuous eavesdropping of a loyal servant, seeking only to serve his master.

15

The Neutral Ground

Cooper's most penetrating and enduring idea in *The Spy* was his development of Scott's descriptions of "the Neutral Ground," the notion of No-Man's-Land's metaphoric relation with modern life. We must be alert to this concept within this novel: it's title is *The Spy, A Tale of the Neutral Ground*. But this is a tale without a hero. A spy cannot be one, Harvey Birch is certainly not a conventional hero. The genuine hero (in the moral lights of 1821) is Dunwoodie, and he only because of his social station: he gets to marry the heroine. Just that configuration of characters puts greater stress on the novel as a tale of the Neutral Ground.

The leader of the Skinners who raze Harvey's house (he is the "speculator" who had offered to buy the dwelling, here in his paramilitary guise) understands the Neutral Ground: "the law of the Neutral Ground is the law of the strongest," he says "with a malignant laugh" (I, 226).

The Neutral Ground in the novel is a specific geographic region—now the area of New York State that is defined, approximately, as Westchester County. After the battle of White Plains (in 1776) the British consolidated in and around New York City, while Washington's forces controlled the region to the north. Cooper describes it thus: "The county of West-Chester ... became common ground, in which both parties continued to act for the remainder of the war of the revolution." The country was "abandoned entirely to the ravages of the miscreants who plundered between both armies, serving neither" (II, 136). A large proportion of its inhabitants, "either restrained by their attachments, or influenced by their fears, affected a neutrality they did not always feel .... Great numbers, however, wore masks, which even to this day have not been thrown aside" (II, 2). Between these armies was an extensive Neutral Ground (in itself a neutral term, not nearly as emotionally loaded as "No-Man's-Land" because of its previously forgotten and subsequently acquired denotations), a region in which armed parties might sally forth, and where irregulars plundered the unwary. The Neutral Ground was originally real estate; but in Cooper it becomes not merely topography but a state of mind.

The Neutral Ground is that "area" which is controlled by neither friend nor enemy, where the environment is especially lethal because there is no control, no lawfulness, and no hierarchy, where the seemingly innocuous inhabitants may prove murderous at any moment. In *The Spy*, the land is fought over by forces from both sides; they do not inhabit the Neutral Ground, but only enter it preparatory to fighting. When the combat is ended, the armies withdraw. Among the Ground's inhabitants are the irregulars of both sides, who are like privateers fighting and pillaging more for personal gain than for political conviction. Thus they are the most dangerous since they seldom wear uniforms (and their loyalties cannot be identified at sight) and are likely to attack any individual or any side so long as they think they might thereby turn a profit. We remember that Paulding, Williams, and Van Wart were praised as great patriots by Washington, but condemned as pirates by Tallmadge.

Cooper's prominent characters who live in this terrain, the Whartons at the Locusts, struggle to maintain neutrality (despite the fiercely held, partisan feelings of both Frances and Sarah). Patriarch Wharton remarks to his guest, Mr. Harper, that he no longer goes to New York to indulge his fondness for his pipe because "the war has made any communications with the city, however innocent in themselves, too dangerous to be risked for so trifling an article as tobacco" (I, 8). He has "dear friends" in both armies, and knows that a victory by either side would result in a personal misfortune (I, 13). The Wharton women owe the maintenance of their life styles to the polite, courteous behavior of both British and Colonial officers. Like all civilians who dwell in this region, they are always vulnerable to the irregulars, the Skinners and the Cow-boys, who at one point do burn the Locusts, as they have razed Harvey Birch's cottage.

Like Cooper, contemporary spy novelists rely heavily on the idea of the No-Man's-Land. Their characters live continually in the Neutral Ground, qualifying Harvey Birch as the grandfather of literary secret agents Alec Leamas, Quiller, and Bernie Sampson—even James Bond. The status of the Neutral Ground is continually shifting according to the winds of political power-and-loss. For Richard Hannay (hero of John Buchan's *The Thirty-Nine Steps*) the Neutral Ground is seemingly cordial England, but where in fact he is continually chased and harassed by the enemy agents of the "Black Stone." Not England, however, but Lisbon and Istanbul were the centers of espionage just prior to World War II, and were so depicted in espionage (and some crime) novels, particularly those of Eric Ambler.

After the end of the war, No-Man's-Land moved again, coursing a brief detour through Vienna, settling in Berlin. A city divided among its conquerors, each zone was continually invaded by agents of "the other side." The erection of the Wall in 1961 further strengthened the political world's perception of it as a No-Man's-Land. East faced West across this concrete and steel barrier, and capitalism was here contiguous with communism; the "warring" ideologies and armies were separated yet in imminent and potentially belligerent contact with each other. The Wall has become the focal point of a pre-1989 No-Man's-Land; at points it is physically a double wall, the soil in between mined, booby-trapped, heavily patrolled by armed guards (often with dogs), covered by searchlights and klaxons at night, and by armed guards all of the time. The Berlin Wall was for us something of what Cooper's Neutral Ground must have been for him and his contemporaries.

Le Carré's *The Spy Who Came in from the Cold* begins and ends at the Berlin Wall; so does Len Deighton's *Berlin Game*, and the other novels in that trilogy *(Mexico Set* and *London Match)* take us there often. *Funeral in Berlin* and *An Expensive Place to Die* also exploit this setting, as does *The Cold War Swap*,

The Man Who Lost the War, The Quiet Dogs, to some extent *The Odessa File,* Ian McEwan's recent *The Innocent,* and dozens of other modern fictions. As the Wall was the focal point of this universally lethal Neutral Ground, the city of Berlin partook noticeably of this quality. The agents of each side frequently passed over to the other zone; tourists had to get special visas to visit the other half-city; but no one could legally remain beyond an officially sanctioned—and restrictive—time limit. The further away from the Wall, the less sinister the quality of life. Outside of Berlin to the east the region was the Republic of East Germany, where the loyalties of the population were uncertain. West Berlin was an enclave; for West Berliners to pass into safer territory they had to travel through (or fly over) the surrounding hostile country.

Berlin, for all the years following World War II, was said to have been roiling in spies; maybe it still is the espionage capital of the world. Again Le Carré has said it best when he has his agent, Alec Leamas, remember the Berlin of his early days, "thronging with second-rate agents." One could, in those days, recruit an agent at a cocktail party, brief him over dinner, and he would be blown by breakfast. It was a nightmare for professionals: dozens of agencies, half of them penetrated, thousands of loose ends, too many leads, too few sources, too little space (1983 rpt. 73).

The transit point between east and west, the navel of these two worlds, had become well known throughout both east and west, curiously by the name given it by the American army: "Checkpoint Charley." This small acreage had assumed gigantic proportions on the mental landscapes of many; it was, for those of us who lived through the 1960s and on, an analogue to Byzantium for Yeats: the still point in a geopolitical gyre, the small point where two conflicting ideologies, two antagonistic national conglomerates, met.

The locution of Cooper (and Scott before him)—the Neutral Ground—does not adequately describe for us this city, this Wall, this checkpoint; it does not convey the tension inherent in this patch of land, nor the danger within its limits. No-Man's-Land, though dating from the fourteenth century, is the term for our time. The Neutral Ground—probably "No-Man's-Land" because of its associations with modern warfare—is the more cogent of these two phrases. In such a mindscape one does not know whom one can trust—if anyone. On what agency, what institution, what abstraction can one rely, commit one's loyalty, one's trust, one's belief, one's self, to defend and protect? When the individual cannot trust anyone or anything, when he or she has no commitment to anything, they are vulnerable to fear, suspicion, paranoia.

In a dramatic moment of détente, in 1989, the Berlin Wall began to be dismantled. Several months later the destruction was complete, the huts at Checkpoint Charley were hauled away by crane, the two Germanys reunited. A potent symbol of the Cold War and of the Neutral Zone—No-Man's-Land— was thus dismantled. Is our world now without such an area? Shortly after this lethal region faded in Berlin, Balkan animosities flared anew. Divided by the Emperor Theodocius I in 395 A.D., the present confederation of Yugoslavia (as was the entire Roman Empire) was separated into Latin and Greek domains. Northern Yugoslavia—Croatia and Slovenia—use the Latin alphabet, the southern republics the Greek. An abyss separates these republics, these peoples, their religion and their traditions. One of their traditions is of mutual hatred and continuing bloodshed. The Balkans, then, is the new No-Man's-Land. Fought over for centuries, fought in for centuries, the Balkans—particularly Yugoslavia—is an area without peace, security, without certitude. Is Macedonia Greek, or Serbian, or Bulgarian ("Western Bulgaria"), or part Albanian? It borders all of them; and within them, within Macedonia itself, are nationalists willing to fight to claim what they believe to be their just territorial rights.

If we understand the resonance, the echoes, the aura of this No-Man's-Land, we can much better understand the Neutral Ground of Cooper and his contemporaries; and we get a sharper appreciation of Cooper's vision. Not by mistake is the novel set largely in that clean well-lighted place, the Locusts, which lies in the midst of the Neutral Ground. This house, and the Whartons' subsequent abode, is both symbolic and actual structure; houses are guardians against the cold. They shelter and protect against the disorderliness, the entropy, the dangers, of the wilds without. So it is with the residents and visitors at "the Locusts." All the spies, innocuous and pernicious, gather there at one time: Harvey, Harper, Henry Wharton, and that insidious dissembler, Wellmere. The innocents are there as well, commingling, often baffled by appearances—as we all are—often unable to tell the harmless from the evil, yet continually struggling toward some sort of reconciliation with an understanding of criminality.

In peacetime there are no overt friends as opposed to enemies, but there are others with friendly or with unfriendly intentions. Away from overt hostilities, attacks will probably not be with murderous weapons, but hostility and congeniality are expressed in more subtle ways. The list of examples is beyond counting.

Cooper's *The Spy* is more than a book about a spy, it is more than about spies, more than an essay in spying, more than a study of clandestinity and its culpability; it is more than all of its segments concatenated. And infused through all is the figure, the death, the character, the legend, of Major André. He is the first cause of this novel; without him this would be an entirely different book—perhaps it would not have been written at all.

E. M. Forster wrote (in *Aspects of the Novel*) that above all a fictional narrative must have as its basic requirement passion: "if he [Scott] had passion he would be a great writer—no amount of clumsiness or artificiality would matter then" (1927 rpt. p. 31). Cooper wrote *The Spy* with some passion, though probably not enough to satisfy Forster. It is not a well-crafted book, it has many of the flaws that some of his severest critics complained about, particularly Mark Twain. One wishes that it were more vigorously composed, that over the years it had held up better. For it is, despite its problems, an interesting book, perhaps an important one. Cooper obviously thought deeply about the psychological problems of the clandestine life, about the nature of spying and the character of its guilt. His is a good story, a relevant tale, for our time as well as his; if only he had told it better.

The plot has something of the quality of a bellows. In the first chapters of the novel, the characters are drawn together at the Locusts. Wharton Sr. and his daughters are there already, of course. Then Harper/Washington rides up out of the night storm, asking for shelter. Henry arrives for his disguised visit;

Wellmere drops by when his unit patrols the immediate area; and Harvey drops by secretly to communicate with Harper, ostensibly to sell his wares as part of his normal mercantile rounds. The battle is fought within sight of the piazza, and that action has brought Dunwoodie and Lawton to the house, as it will soon draw Dr. Sitgreaves. Soon enough this unity begins to disintegrate as each of the characters breaks away to pursue his own destiny. Then the dissipation, the expansion of the bellows. Harper has been at the estate to get certain information from Harvey, and after he communicates with his agent, he departs. Harvey leaves on his rounds, whether clandestine or as part of his cover is immaterial for this aspect of the plot. The battle draws Dunwoodie temporarily away from the house, and its aftermath brings Isabella Singleton to it. For a moment only; she is soon to die. Lawton will ride off to his military duties, Dr. Sitgreaves with him, Henry will eventually escape back to his own lines, and the house itself, the Locusts, is soon to be destroyed. The Whartons and their immediate satellites will then move elsewhere, completely disintegrating the plot's geographical compactness.

The problems with the character of Harvey Birch have been discussed throughout. Cooper's readership was not ready for a spy to be a hero; like Natty Bumppo after him, Birch was not a suitable romantic interest. In fact, he was less acceptable than the uncouth woodsman. Yet he is the spy of the title; he is one of the noblest characters in the book. Washington/Harper enters the novel with that reputation already established; Birch must earn our respect, during the course of the action, for his patriotism, his good character.

This is not a novel in which characters develop. Washington is as noble in the opening pages as he will be throughout, Henry Wharton as innocent and full of boyish enthusiasm and naïveté, Wellmere is consistently sarcastic and dissembling, and Harvey is a dedicated patriot and astute secret agent from the first pages to the last. Things happen to all of the characters, but more of them—and those more traumatic—happen to Harvey. He deals with circumstances more or less adeptly, always successfully. Each succeeding event in his life—his captures, his continual traveling, his coping with his father's death and with the Skinners, the destruction of his house, helping Henry escape—each event reinforces what we come to know about him; he does not grow throughout this novel, but our understanding of him does.

As this book is about one spy particularly, it is about all spies. Cooper wants to know, and he wants us to know, what is criminal about the act of espionage as he knew it; disguises can be for perfectly harmless and domestic activities, and they can be employed for nefarious intentions. Everybody in modern life, as in Cooper's time and well before, has secrets; on her deathbed Isabella Singleton gasps that a woman's "life is one of concealed emotions" (II, p. 121). Again, it is no coincidence that respectable Henry Wharton finds it necessary to disguise himself so that he may visit his sisters and their aging father; and later, to escape from an unjust imprisonment out of uniform. Harvey, the real spy as we think of that role, is socially disreputable, a landless itinerant peddler, while the aristocratic and noble Harper/Washington appears in disguise for patriotic purposes. His intentions are by no means innocent (especially for the other side), but they are nevertheless, for Americans, commendable. Wellmere's disguise is of a different kind; always in uniform, always spouting about his fulfilled duty to his king, he is a moral reprobate. He deceives as consciously as does Harvey, but not in the cause of country or prince; Wellmere's deceptions are on behalf of his personal lusts. The colonel has meanly sinned against his fellows. Cooper concludes his exploration of disguise and dissembling and deceit and treachery in such cases with the verdict of guilty. All the others—Henry, Harvey, Harper—are to one degree or another justifiable.

And André: Cooper was a patriot, and has written (in *Notions*) of Washington's justification in ordering the major's execution. But Cooper, as did thousands of Americans, greatly admired the Englishman. *The Spy* is the novelist's partial vindication of André. The unfortunate major was as culpable as was Birch and Harper, but like them, he served an honorable cause. Unfortunately, André's most vocal supporter was Colonel Wellmere, though his platitudinous defenses were only disguised attacks on the Americans. André's most persuasive support comes from the situation as well as from the rhetoric of Henry Wharton, who finds himself, though innocent, in André's predicament. Wharton's innocence is unassailable, but is André's? We would not think their situations analogous, or the major entirely guiltless; but Cooper's alignment of their plights lessens, by analogy, the unfortunate major's criminality. He was lawfully serving his king, was not voluntarily out of uniform, did not get captured behind the enemy's "lines," his trial was only questionably fair and just. We, along with Cooper, admire him because when caught, André told the truth; while imprisoned, he behaved with model bravery and composure.

In Harvey Birch, Cooper was able to give full scope to his insights into the nature of the clandestine life. Harvey is the novel's only full-time, professional spy, and his diminished social standing allows his creator to explore, with safety, his weaknesses, and the psychological problems inherent in the role. In 1821 what spies existed were not known to the public; little was known about spying at all, and very few thought about espionage in any methodical way. That public had only briefly considered and certainly fixed notions of spies and of spying—if they thought about the matter at all. Cooper's insights into the clandestine life, therefore, would have been scarcely noticed, and in fact none of the reviews of *The Spy* mention this aspect. Maybe glimpses into the lives of spies were not thought worthy for either literature or its critics. But Cooper tells us something both interesting and obvious (to us, now) about Harvey's life: he is lonely, and he yearns for recognition. These life hazards are made known when Harvey laments the death of his father. He will be lonely. This is obvious, yet it is fresh news; spies are lonely, they tell us so, and occasionally the heroes of spy novels are afflicted with loneliness. But it was not obvious in 1821, and Cooper deserves credit for having seen that it would be. And he also saw that people want credit for their accomplishments, they want praise and support when they perform their assignments, especially when those jobs are well executed. Harvey dreaded dying with his deeds and his patriotism unsung; he wanted his loyalty and his convictions to be recognized by his countrymen—he had given up too much of himself on their behalf not to ask for that—but he was too dedicated a patriot to break that deepest of his covers. Hence his inner conflict, hence Cooper's insight;

it may have been more than a century premature, but Cooper's recognition, like Harvey's, is due.

As the prevailing attitudes toward the conduct of war were defined, being out of uniform did not necessarily connote guilt. If it did, Henry Wharton would certainly be guilty (as he is, technically, in the novel); but Cooper allows him to escape—with Birch's help—and the reader certainly feels his innocence, despite the outward appearance of his situation. Harper/Washington is also out of uniform, but he never enters the enemy's lines—the only time we see him is in the Neutral Ground—though in his capacity as field officer servicing a spy who is operating against the British. On the same moot grounds as those used in the André affair, the enemy might well execute him if captured. Harvey Birch is clearly and legally a spy, operating behind enemy lines (he frequently went into New York), always dissimulating, always with the intent of transmitting information to the rebels, the "other side." Yet a twentieth-century reader must find him admirable; if anything, Birch is too dedicated, too committed to his cause, to be completely believable. Yet he is too much a part of the shadow world to be sympathetic.

Colonel Wellmere never doffs his uniform, never intends to give information to the enemy; but he is the most disreputable character in this novel. Wellmere's dissembling is in the interest of his own passions, not for any transcendent commitments or for the sake of his country. And while his identity is not determined by his attire, he is nevertheless a character of appearances: he has lied about himself and his marital status so that he may seduce one of the Wharton women. Like Birch, Wellmere has disguised his intentions; but unlike the motivations of the peddler, they are not for a transcendent or a noble cause. Wellmere is the one disreputable spy in Cooper's novel. When his bigamous intentions have been exposed by Birch, the colonel declares that the laws of his country will never compel him to abide by the claims of his recently wed English wife. Lawton rejoins, "but will not conscience, and the laws of God?" (II, p. 81).

Spying in itself is not evil, the author has realized, but he insists that one must have a high moral motivation for clandestine activity. The end may justify the means. In a conversation with Katy Haynes, Sarah defends her brother, Henry, against the casual charge that he is said to be a spy, and that one spy is as bad as another. "`'Tis false,'" she exclaims, "her eyes lighting with extraordinary animation, `no act of deception is worthy of my brother, nor of any would he be guilty, for so base a purpose as gain or promotion'" (II, pp. 138-39). Seen this way, Birch—the spy of the book's title—is a loyal and dedicated patriot; Wellmere an immoral dissembler. There is a great moral difference depicted here; and Cooper was a moralist.

REFERENCES

Anon. *The National Intelligencer.* 4 March 1817.

Anon. 1865. *Andreana. Containing the Trial, Execution and Various Matter Connected with the History of Major John André.* Philadelphia: Horace, W. Smith. [Huntington Library accession #68034].

Anon. 1874. *Andreana: Appendix to Sargent's Andre.* 2 vols. Huntington Library accession #1378.

Anon. 1882. "The Secret Service of the Revolution." *Magazine of American History.*

Arnold, Charles Henry. 1782. *The New and Impartial Universal History of North and South America, and of the Present Trans-Atlantic War.* London: Alexander Hagg.

Beard, James Franklin, ed. 1960. *The Letters and Journals of James Fenimore Cooper.* Vol. I. Cambridge, MA: Harvard University Press.

Cawelti, John G. N.D. *The Six-Gun Mystique.* Bowling Green, OH: Bowling Green University Popular Press.

Cooper, James Fenimore. 1821. *The Spy; a Tale of the Neutral Ground.* 2 vols. New York: Wiley and Halstead.

———. 1828. *Notions of the Americans.* 2 vols. London: Henry Colburn.

———. 1971. *The Spy: A Tale of the Neutral Ground.* Ed. James H. Pickering. Schenectady: New College and University Press.

———. 1982 rpt. *Gleanings in Europe, Switzerland.* Eds. Robert Spiller and James F. Beard. Albany, N.Y.: State University of New York Press. Originally published as *Sketches of Switzerland.*

Decker, Malcolm. 1959. *Ten Days of Infamy*. New York: Arno Press.
Dunlap, William. 1799. *André: A Tragedy in Five Acts*. London: David Ogilvy and Son. [Huntington Library accession #KD-350].
Essex, Earl of. 1643. *Laws and Ordinances of Warre, Established for the better Conduct of the ARMY*. London: Luke Fawne.
Flexner, James T. 1953. *The Traitor and the Spy*. Boston: Little, Brown & Co.
Forster, E. M. 1927 rpt. *Aspects of the Novel*. New York: Harcourt, Brace, & Co.
Greene, Edward Burnaby. 1782. *The Prophecy of Andree: An Ode: Written in the Year 1780*. London: G. Kearsly.
Gregg, Josiah. 1967 rpt. *The Commerce of the Prairies*. Lincoln: University of Nebraska Press.
Grossman, James. 1949. *James Fenimore Cooper*. New York: William Sloan Associates.
Grotius, Hugo. 1682. *The Rights of War and Peace*. Trans. William Evats. 3 vols. London: [M. W. for Thomas Basset].
Hall, Harrison. 1826. *Illustrations from The Spy, The Pioneers, and The Waverly Novels, with Explanatory and Critical Remarks*. Philadelphia: The Port Folio Office. [Huntington Library prints (various subjects) #442522].
Hatch, Robert McConnell. 1986. *Major John André: A Gallant in Spy's Clothing*. Boston: Houghton Mifflin Co.
Holloway, Charlotte Molyneux. 1889 rpt. *Nathan Hale: The Martyr-Hero of the Revolution*. 1902. New York: F. Tennyson Neely.
Johnston, Henry Phelps. 1901. *Nathan Hale, 1776: Biography and Memorials*. New York: [Privately printed].
Kahn, David. 1978. *Hitler's Spies: German Military Intelligence During World War II*. New York: Macmillan Publishing Co.
Le Carré, John. 1983 rpt. *The Spy Who Came in from the Cold*. New York: Bantam Books.
Leisy, Ernest Ervin. 1929. *American Literature: An Interpretive Survey*. New York: Thomas Y. Crowell Co.
Lodge, Henry Cabot, ed. *André's Journal*. 1903. 2 vols. Boston: The Bibliophile Society.
McDowell, Tremaine. 1930. "James Fenimore Cooper as Self-critic." *Studies in Philology* 27:513-14.

Nevius, Blake. 1976. *Cooper's Landscapes*. Berkeley: University of California Press.

⚝ Odell, George C. D. 1927. *Annals of the New York Stage*. 2 vols. New York: Columbia University Press.

Pattie, James O. 1984 rpt. *The Personal Narrative of James O. Pattie*. 1831. Lincoln: University of Nebraska Press.

Peacham, Henry. 1622. *The Compleat Gentleman*. London.

Peck, H. Daniel. 1977. *A World by Itself*. New Haven: Yale University Press.

Puddicombe, John Newell. 1782. *The British Hero in Captivity. A Poem. Dedicated to His Royal Highness the Prince of Wales*. London: J. Robson.

Railton, Stephen. 1978. *Fenimore Cooper: A Study in his Life and Imagination*. Princeton, NJ: Princeton University Press.

Ringe, Donald A. 1962. *James Fenimore Cooper*. New York: Twain Publishers.

_____. 1977. "The Spy in the Context of Other Contemporary Novels of the American Revolution." *American Literature*. 49:352-65.

Rosenberg, Bruce. 1974. *Custer and the Epic of Defeat*. State College: Penn State University Press.

St. Armand, Barton Levi. 1978. "Harvey Birch as the Wandering Jew: Literary Calvanism in James Fenimore Cooper's *The Spy*." *American Literature* 50:348-68.

Sargent, Winthrop. 1902. *The Life and Career of Major John André, Adjutant-General of the British Army in America*. Ed., William Abbatt. New York: William Abbatt.

_____, ed. 1904. *Major André's Journal*. Tarrytown: William Abbatt.

⚝ Seymour, George Dudley. 1941. *Documentary Life of Nathan Hale: Comprising All Available Official and Private Documents Bearing on the Life of the Patriot*. New Haven: Tuttle, Morehouse & Taylor Co.

Smith, Henry Nash. 1970. *Virgin Land. The American West as Symbol and Myth*. Cambridge, MA: Harvard University Press.

Spiller, Robert and James F. Beard. 1980. *Sketches of Switzerland*. Albany, N.Y.: The State University of New York Press.

Originally published by Cooper as *Gleanings of Europe, Switzerland.*

Tillotson, Harry Stanton. 1948. *The Beloved Spy: The Life and Loves of Major John André.* Caldwell, ID: The Caxton Printers, Ltd.

𝄪 Van Doren, Carl. 1941. *Secret History of the American Revolution.* New York: The Viking Press.

Walker, Warren S. 1962. *James Fenimore Cooper: An Introduction and Interpretation.* New York: Barnes and Noble.

⸺. 1981. "Cooper's Fictional Use of the Oral Tradition" in *James Fenimore Cooper: His Country and His Art.* Ed. George A. Test. Oneonta, N Y: State University College.

Wallace, James D. 1986. *Early Cooper and His Audience.* New York: Columbia University Press.

Ward, Robert. 1639. *Animadversions of Warre; Or, A Militarie Magazine.* London: John Dawson.

MANUSCRIPTS

William Keeney Bixby Collection, Huntington Library #X 68034.

The McDonald Collection at the Huguenot Historical Society, New Rochelle, N.Y.

Major André Collection, Huntington Library #68034.

Nathaniel Greene Papers, transcripts in the Huntington Library. [No specific accession number; several hundred items are included in this collection, numbered according to letter or item.] Originals in the Library of Congress, National Archives.

Index

André — A Tragedy in Five Acts, 56
Ambler, Eric, 83, 137
André, Major John: ("Anderson, John," "John Andrews" and "J. A. Anderson"), 1, 3-7, 9-14, 15-17, 19-25, 27-39, 41-50, 51-59, 63-67, 69-70, 73-76, 84, 101, 108-111, 118, 122-126, 129, 131-132, 140, 142-144
Arnold, General Benedict: ("Gustavus" and "Gustavus letter"), 9-11, 14, 15-17, 23-24, 27-39, 41, 44-47, 49-50, 51, 54-55, 63, 65, 67, 108, 123
Averill, Charles, 80

Balkans, The, 139
Bates, Ann, 32, 84, 109-110
Berlin Wall, 98, 137, 139
Bill, Buffalo, 80
Birch, Harvey, 43, 70, 75-76, 79-80, 83-85, 95, 97, 99-100, 108-111, 113, 115-119, 121-122, 124, 126, 130-133, 135, 137, 141-145
Bond, James, 97, 137
Boone, Daniel, 79
Buchan, John, 83, 97, 100, 137
Bumppo, Natty (Leatherstocking, Derslayer), 116, 141

Caesar, 113, 122, 124, 129, 133
Calquhoun, Joseph (Calhoon), 35-36
Calquhoun, Samuel (Calhoon), 35-36
Carlisle, Penna, 23
Cawelti, John, 79, 81
Checkpoint Charley, 98, 138-139
Childers, Erskine, 96
Clinton, General Henry, 13, 16, 25, 27, 30-31, 33-37, 48-49, 58, 68, 110, 116
Colonel Wellmere, 75, 107, 119, 126-130, 133, 140-142, 144-145
Continental Army, 3, 22, 28, 32, 37, 48, 123
Cooper, Susan, 73, 80
Cow-boys, 17, 38, 41, 116, 131-132, 137

De Lancey, Elizabeth, 76
De Lancey, Oliver, 76, 115
De Lancey, Thomas James, 54
Deighton, Len, 137
Dunwoodie, Major, 80, 100, 117-118, 120, 123-124, 126-128, 130-131, 135, 141

Essex, Earl of, 12

Forster, E M, 140
Franks, Rebecca, 23

Geneva, 12, 19, 66
Goldman, William, 97
Goodrich, Andrew Thompson, 71-72
Greene, General Nathaniel, 11, 15-17, 47, 50
Greene, Grahame, 96
Gregg, Josiah, 78
Grey, General Charles, 20, 24-25
Grotius, Hugo, 12

Hale, Nathan, 49, 67-70, 108
Hamilton, Alexander, 4, 14, 15, 17, 47-48, 52
HMS *Vulture*, 4, 34

Invisible ink, 28-29

jargon code, 29

King, Lieutenant Joshua, 43, 46-48

Laune, Peter, 3-4, 6
Lawton, Captain Jack, 116-121, 128, 131-132, 141, 144

Le Carré, John, 83, 98-100, 137-138
Locusts, The, 113, 115-117, 120, 122-123, 128-131, 133, 136-137, 139-141

Mabie Tavern, 3, 5
McDonald, Dr. J. M., 58, 87-93

Neutral Ground, 9, 13, 30, 37-39, 42-43, 47-48, 75, 83-85, 87, 91-92, 95-98, 106, 109-111, 114, 121-122, 124-125, 135-139, 144
No-Man's-Land, 42, 85, 88, 95-98, 106, 135-139
Notions of the Americans, 41, 51, 63, 65, 73

Odell, Reverend Jonathan, 27, 29-31, 34, 59

Pattie, Joseph, 77-78
Paulding, John, 14, 41, 43, 132, 136
Philadelphia, 16, 19, 21-25, 51, 110
Precaution, 71-72, 105, 107

Quebec City, 21

Robinson, Colonel Beverly, 10, 34-36, 44, 49
Russell, Major Benjamin, 6

Scammel, Colonel Alexander, 4, 6
Scott, Sir Walter, 95, 106, 135, 138, 140
Seward, Anna, 20, 52

Index

Shippen, Peggy, 23, 27-28
Singleton, Isabella, 128, 141-142
Sitgreaves, Dr., 128-129, 141
Skinners, 43, 63, 91, 93, 116-117, 130-132, 135, 137, 141
Smith, Henry Nash, 79-80
Smith, Joshua, 35-39, 47, 50
Sneyd, Honora, 20-21
Spy, The, 43, 51, 57, 63, 65, 70-72, 73-75, 79, 83-85, 96, 98-101, 103, 105-107, 109-111, 132, 135-137, 140-143, 145
Spy Novel, The, 83, 96, 100
Stansburg, Joseph ("Jonathan Stevens"), 29

Tallmadge, Major Benjamin, 6, 32, 34, 42-46, 48, 76-77, 88, 136
Tappan (Camp Tappan), 3, 14, 15-16, 25, 59, 73
Tarrytown (Tarry Town), 9, 39
Thatcher, Dr. James, 3, 5-7
Townsend, Robert ("Culper Junior"), 77
Turner, Frederick Jackson, 81

Van Wart, Isaac, 41-43, 63, 136
Victor, Orville, 80

Ward, Robert, 13
Washington, George (Mr. Harper), 3-4, 6, 9-14, 16-17, 19, 32, 38, 43-47, 49-50, 51-54, 58, 65, 67-69, 73, 75-76, 83-84, 99-100, 107, 109-111, 113, 115-116, 119-126, 131-133, 135-136, 140-142, 144
West Point, 10, 13, 15-16, 28, 30-32, 36-38, 44, 46-47, 57
Western, The, 36, 80-82
Westminster Abbey, 59, 108
Wharton, Frances, 80, 84, 111, 115-116, 122-129, 131, 136, 140-144
Wharton, Henry, 65, 75, 80, 84, 95, 100, 111, 115-116, 118, 122-129, 131, 136, 140-144
Wharton, Sarah, 65, 75, 84, 111, 115-116, 122-129, 131, 136, 140-144
Williams, David, 14, 41-43, 136
Woodhull, Abraham ("Culper Senior"), 77

About the Author

BRUCE A. ROSENBERG is currently Professor of American Civilization at Brown University. He is the author of numerous books on American culture, among them *Folklore and Literature* (1991); *The Code of the West* (1982); *Custer and the Epic Defeat* (1974); and *The Art of the American Folk Preacher* (winner of the James Russell Lowell Prize, 1970). He is also co-author of *Ian Fleming* (1989) and *The Spy Story* (1987).

**Recent Titles in
Contributions to the Study of Popular Culture**

Master Space: Film Images of Capra, Lubitsch, Sternberg, and Wyler
Barbara Bowman

The Cosby Show: Audiences, Impact, and Implications
Linda K. Fuller

America's Musical Pulse: Popular Music in Twentieth-Century Society
Kenneth J. Bindas, editor

Not Just for Children: The Mexican Comic Book in the Late 1960s and 1970s
Harold E. Hinds, Jr., and Charles M. Tatum

Creating the Big Game: John W. Heisman and the Invention of American Football
Wiley Lee Umphlett

"Mr. B" Or Comforting Thoughts About the Bison: A Critical Biography of Robert Benchley
Wes D. Gehring

Religion and Sport: The Meeting of Sacred and Profane
Charles S. Prebish

Songs of Love and Death: The Classical American Horror Film of the 1930s
Michael Sevastakis

Hollywood as Mirror: Changing Views of "Outsiders" and "Enemies" in American Movies
Robert Brent Toplin, editor

Radical Visions: American Film Renaissance, 1967–1976
Glenn Man

Stanley Kubrick: A Narrative and Stylistic Analysis
Mario Falsetto

Ethnicity and Sport in North American History and Culture
George Eisen and David Wiggins, editors

HARDCOVER BAR CODE